How to
EMBROIDER
Almost
Every Cute Thing

TSUKAERU ONE POINT SHISHU 550 (NV70572)
Copyright ©2020 NIHON VOGUE-SHA
Photography by Yukari Shirai
All rights reserved.

Original Japanese edition published by NIHON VOGUE Corp.
English language rights, translation & production by World Book Media, LLC
Email: info@worldbookmedia.com

First published in the United States of America in 2022 by Quarry Books, an imprint of
The Quarto Group
100 Cummings Center
Suite 265-D
Beverly, Massachusetts 01915-6101
Telephone: (978) 282-9590
Fax: (978) 283-2742
Quarto.com

Quarry Books titles are also available at discount for retail, wholesale, promotional, and bulk
purchase. For details, contact the Special Sales Manager by email at specialsales@quarto.com
or by mail at The Quarto Group, Attn: Special Sales Manager, 100 Cummings Center, Suite
265-D, Beverly, MA 01915-6101. USA.

10 9 8 7 6 5 4 3 2 1

ISBN: 978-0-7603-7750-5

Printed in China

How to
EMBROIDER
Almost
Every Cute Thing

A Sourcebook of **550**
Motifs + Beginner Stitch Tutorials

By Nihon Vogue

27

43

14

29

8   17

contents

24

44

38

44

Assorted Patterns

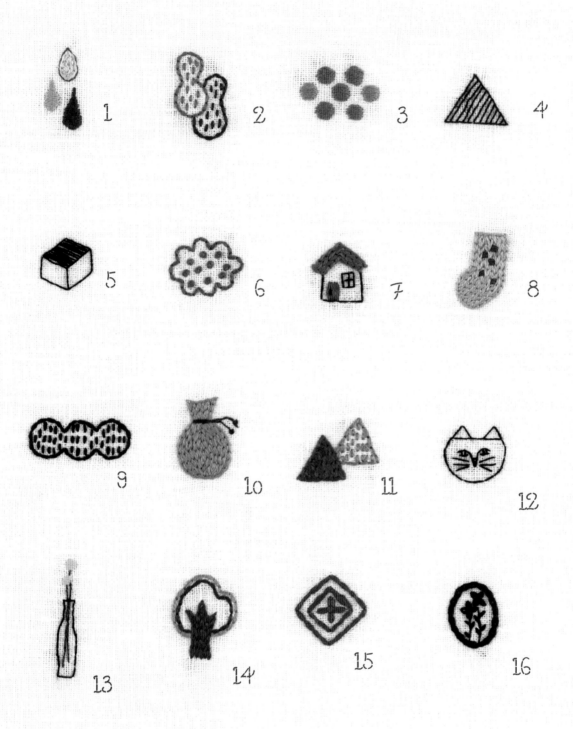

1

2

3

4

5

6

7

8

9

10

11

12

13

14

15

16

Instructions: Pages 56–57
Design & Embroidery: nekogao

Simple Flowers

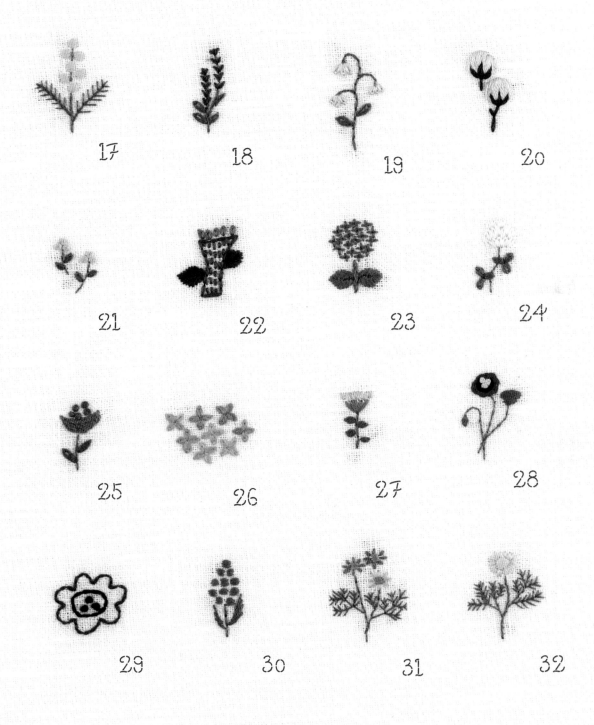

17

18

19

20

21

22

23

24

25

26

27

28

29

30

31

32

Instructions: Pages 58–59
Design & Embroidery: nekogao

Folk Art Flowers

33   34   35   36

37   38   39   40

41   42   43   44

45   46   47   48

Instructions: Pages 60–63
Design & Embroidery: nico.

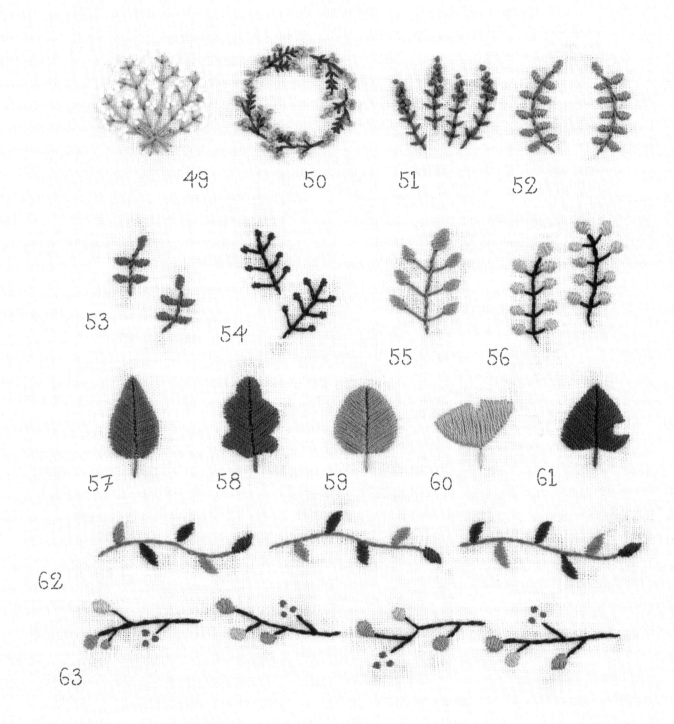

49 50 51 52

53 54 55 56

57 58 59 60 61

62

63

Fairytale Flowers

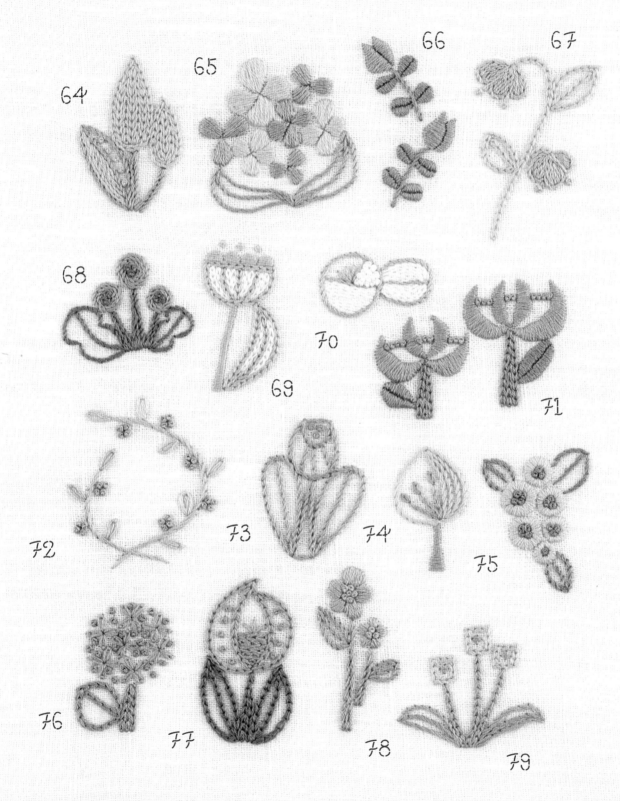

64

65

66

67

68

69

70

71

72

73

74

75

76

77

78

79

Instructions: Pages 64–67

Design & Embroidery: ironna happa

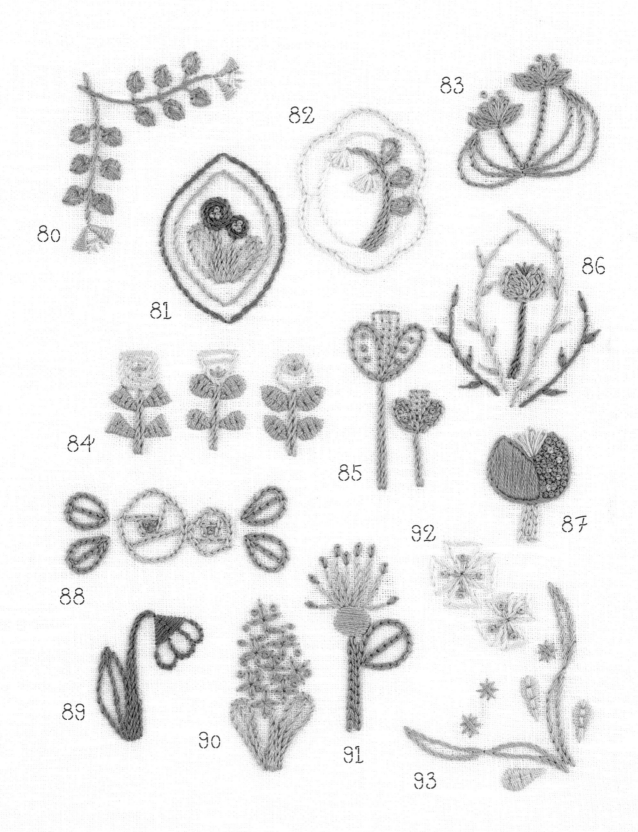

80

82

83

81

86

84

85

92

87

88

89

90

91

93

Breakfast Foods

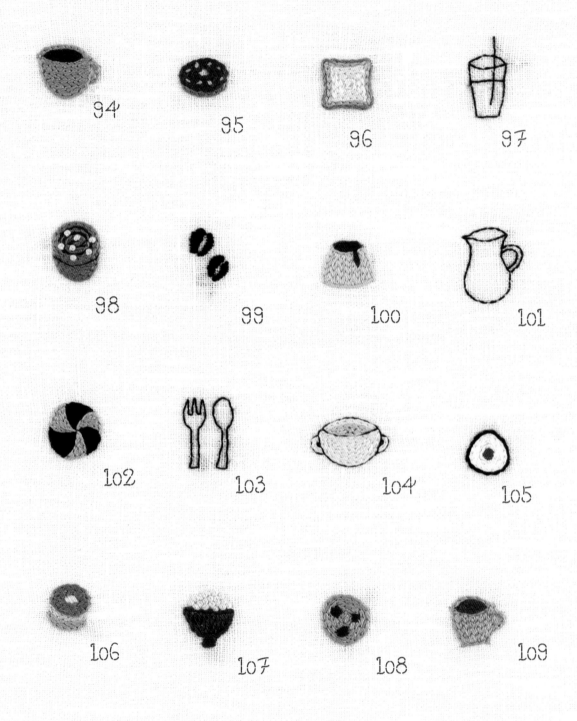

94

95

96

97

98

99

100

101

102

103

104

105

106

107

108

109

Instructions: Pages 68–69
Design & Embroidery: nekogao

Fruits & Vegetables

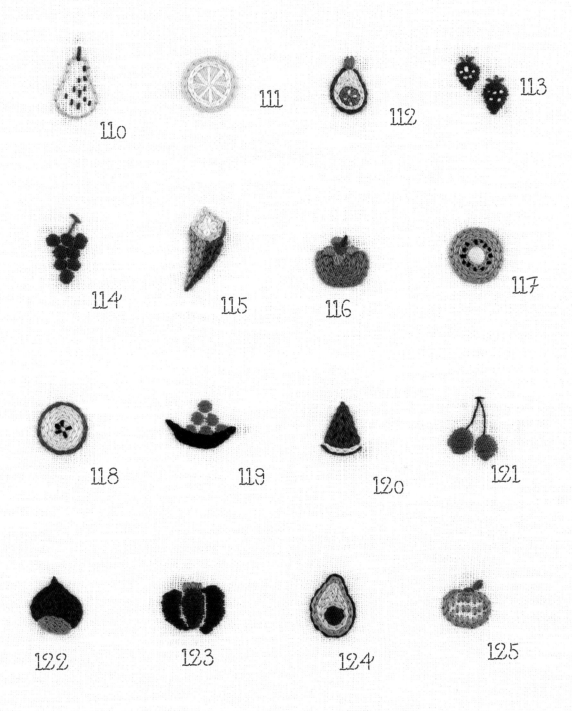

110

111

112

113

114

115

116

117

118

119

120

121

122

123

124

125

Instructions: Pages 70–71
Design & Embroidery: nekogao

Favorite Foods

126

127

128

129

130

131

132

133

134

135

136

137

138

139

140

141

Instructions: Pages 72–73
Design & Embroidery: pulpy.

14

Sweets & Treats

142

143

144

145

146

147

148

149

150

151

152

153

154

155

156

157

Instructions: Pages 74–75
Design & Embroidery: pulpy。

Zodiac Animals

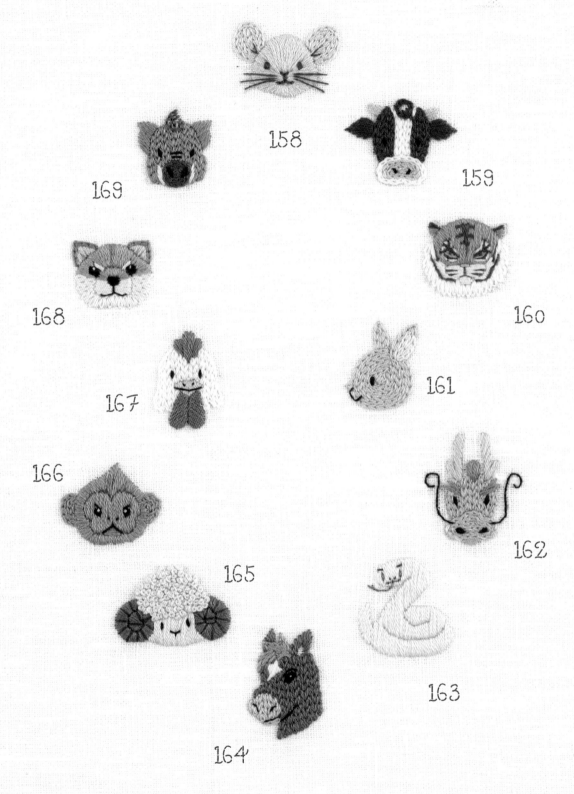

158

169

159

168

160

167

161

166

162

165

163

164

Instructions: Pages 76–77
Design & Embroidery: Chicchi

Dogs & Cats

170

171

172

173

176

174

175

177

178

179

180

181

182

183

184

185

Instructions: Pages 78–79
Design & Embroidery: Chicchi

Favorite Animals

186

187

188

189

190

191

192

193

194

195

196

197

198

199

200

201

Instructions: Pages 80–83
Design & Embroidery: Chicchi

202

203

204

205

206

207

208

209

210

211

212

213

214

215

216

217

Animal Friends

218

219

220

221

222

223

224

225

226

227

228

229

230

231

232

233

Instructions: Pages 84–87
Design & Embroidery: mopsi

234

235

236

237

238

239

240

241

242

243

244

245

246

247

248

249

Fairytale Animals

250

251

252

253

254

255

256

257

258

Instructions: Pages 88–91
Design & Embroidery: arinocosha

259

260

261

262

263

264

265

266

267

More Fairytale Animals

268

269

270

272

271

273

274

275

276

Instructions: Pages 92–95

Design & Embroidery: arinocosha

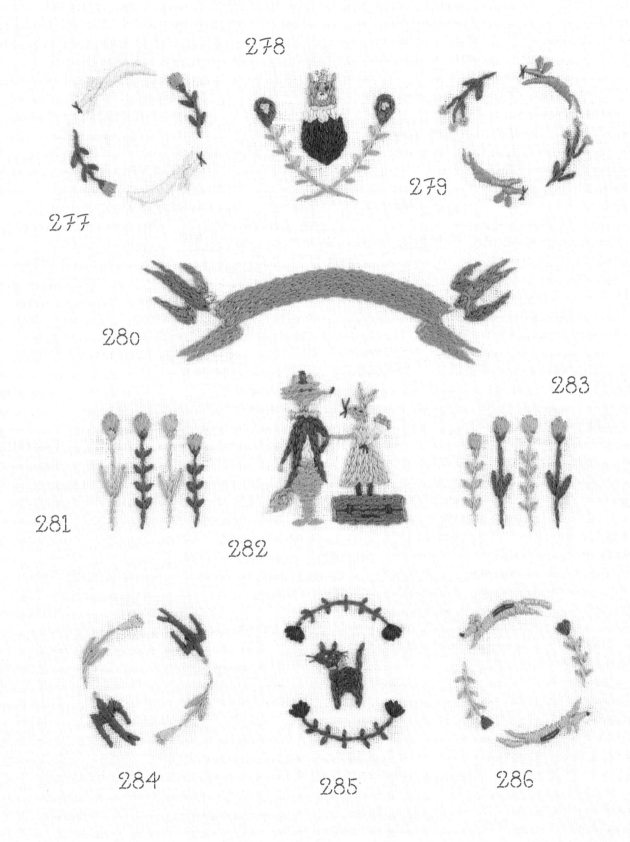

278

277

279

280

283

281

282

284   285   286

Everyday Life

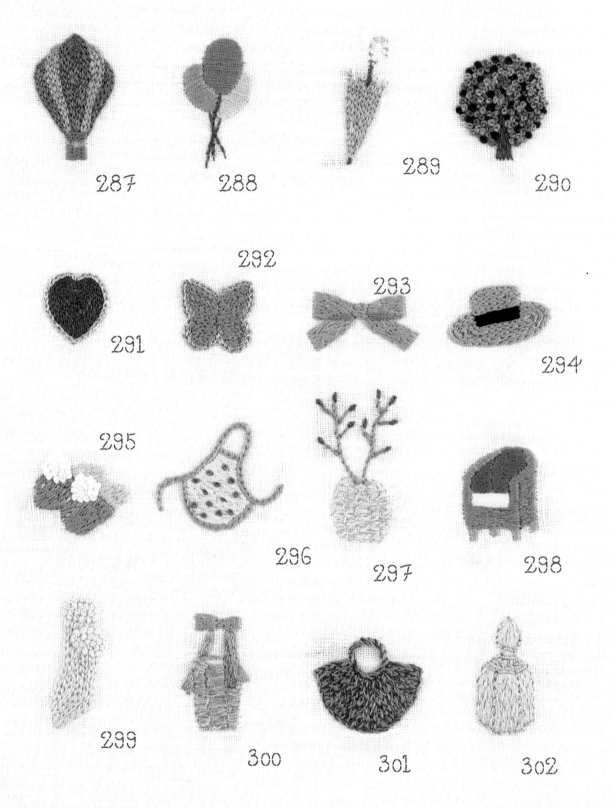

287

288

289

290

291

292

293

294

295

296

297

298

299

300

301

302

Instructions: Pages 96–99
Design & Embroidery: TRÈS JOLIE

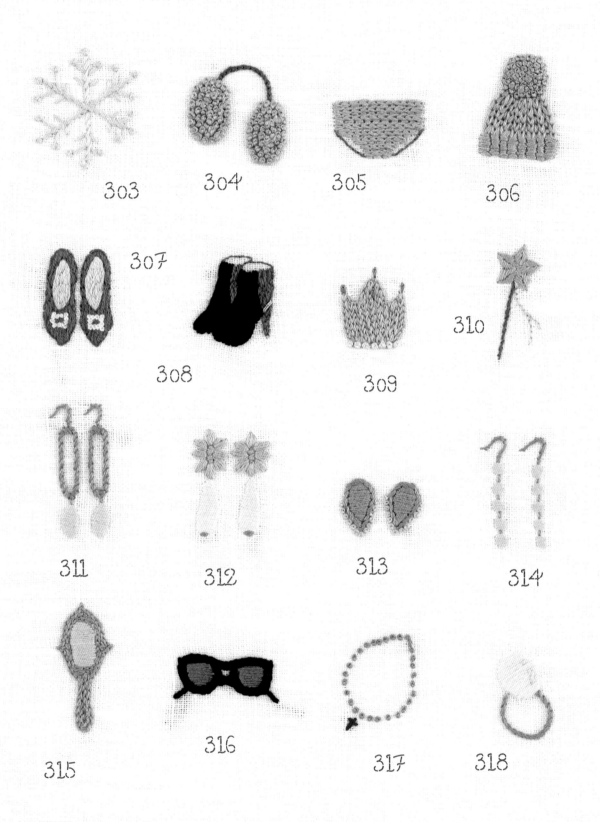

303

304

305

306

307

308

309

310

311

312

313

314

315

316

317

318

Sports & Games

319

320 We love base ball!

321

322

323

324

325 Goal!

326

327 Attack!!

328

329

330 Volley 4 ball

331

332 BASKET 7 BALL

333

334 One for All All for One

Instructions: Pages 100–103
Design & Embroidery: Chicchi

335

336

337

Let's ping-pong

338

339

340

Victory

341

342

343

344

345

346

smash!

347

348

349

RUGBY

350

351
352
353
354
355
356
357
358
359
360
361
362
363

Instructions: Pages 104–107
Design & Embroidery: Chicchi

Border Designs

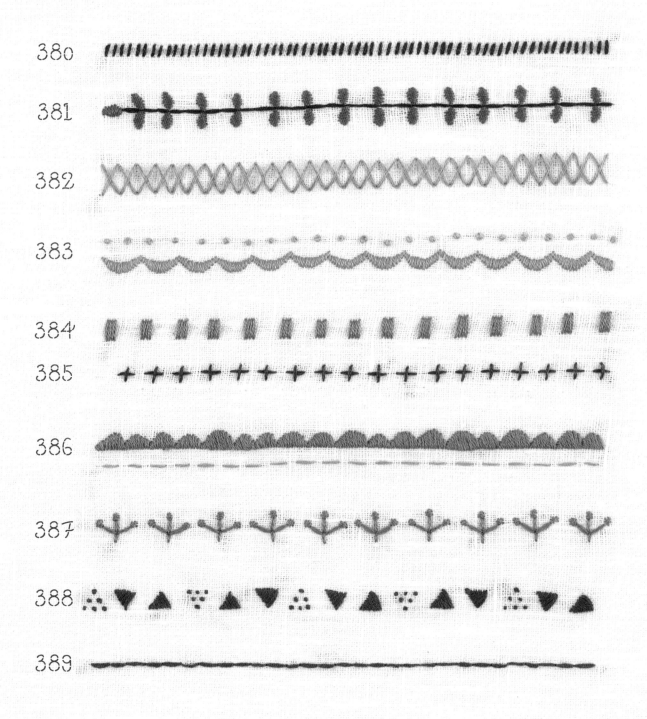

380
381
382
383
384
385
386
387
388
389

Instructions: Pages 108–111
Design & Embroidery: nico.

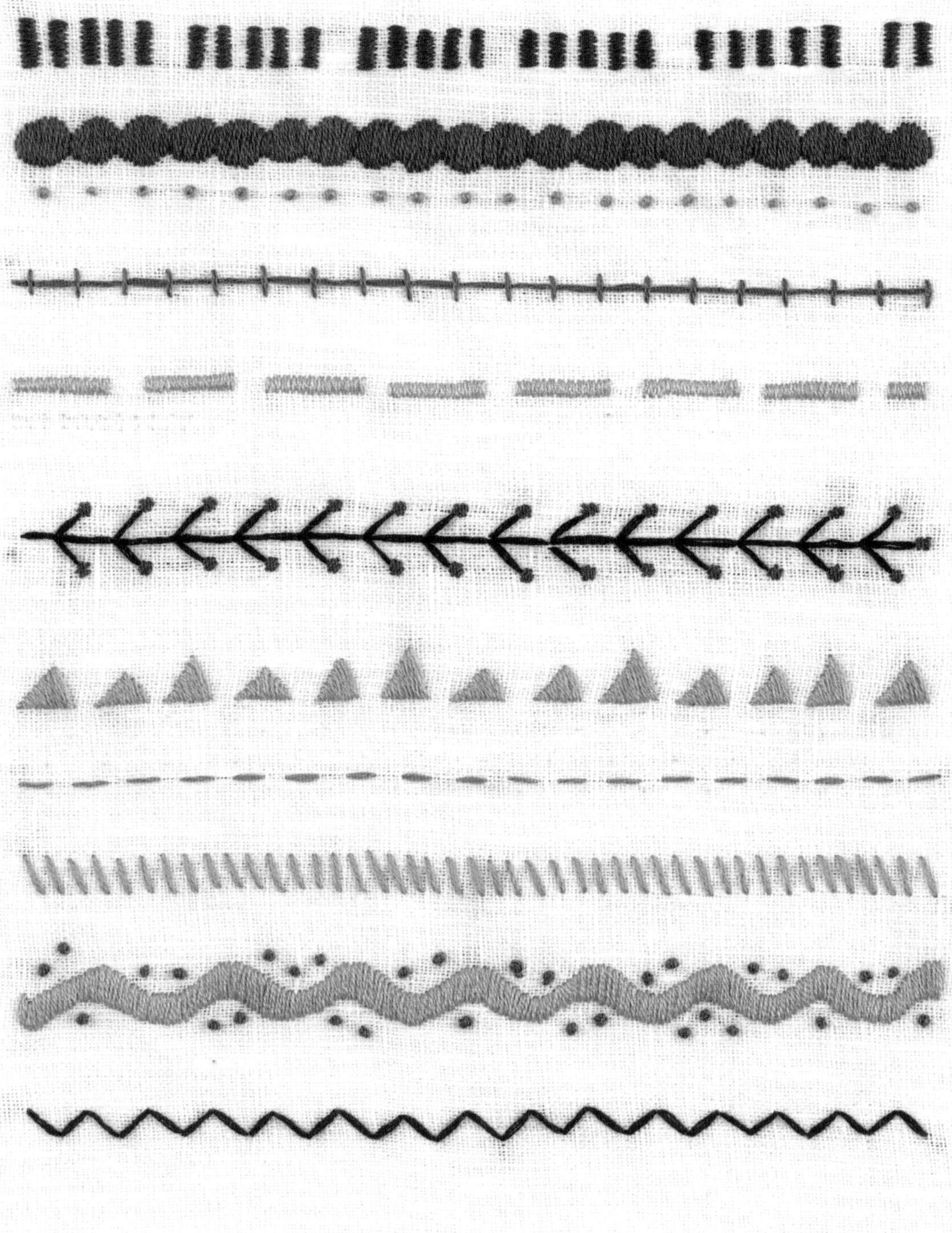

390

391

392

393

394

395

396

397

398

399

Flower Alphabets

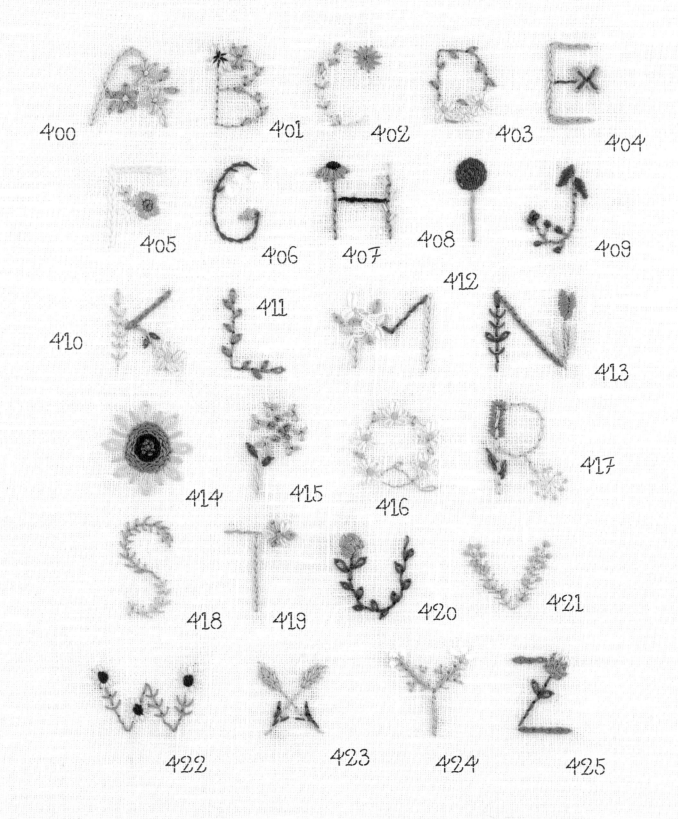

400

401

402

403

404

405

406

407

408

409

410

411

412

413

414

415

416

417

418

419

420

421

422

423

424

425

Instructions: Pages 112–115
Design & Embroidery: Ray chel*

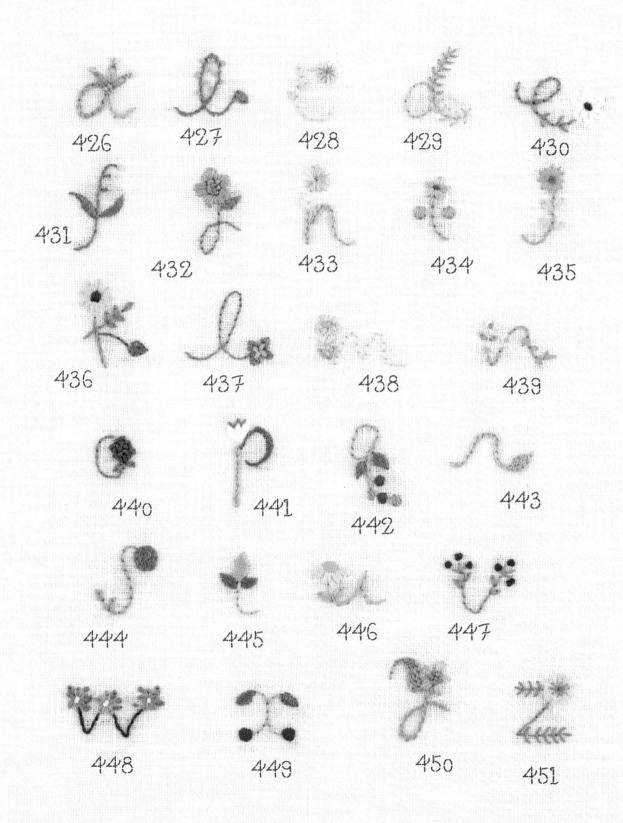

426 427 428 429 430

431 432 433 434 435

436 437 438 439

440 441 442 443

444 445 446 447

448 449 450 451

Food Alphabets

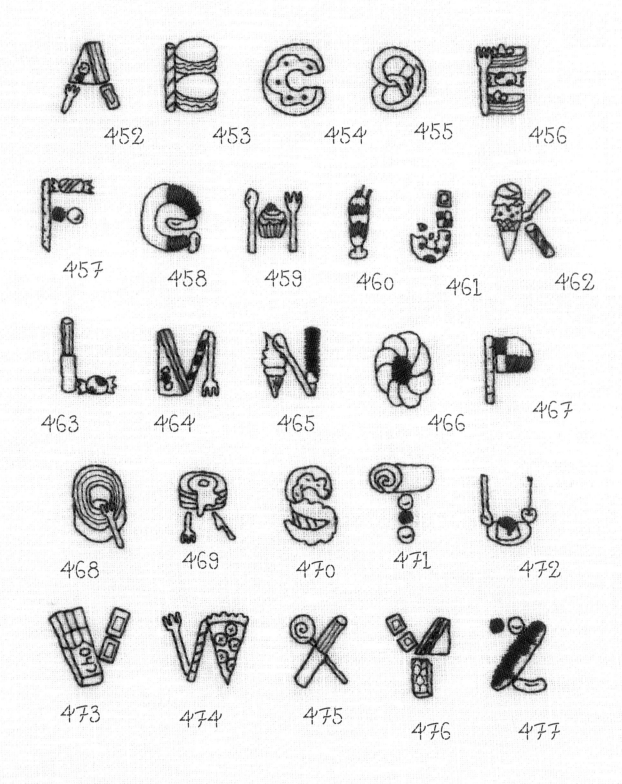

452 453 454 455 456

457 458 459 460 461 462

463 464 465 466 467

468 469 470 471 472

473 474 475 476 477

Instructions: Pages 116–119

Design & Embroidery: Kumamori

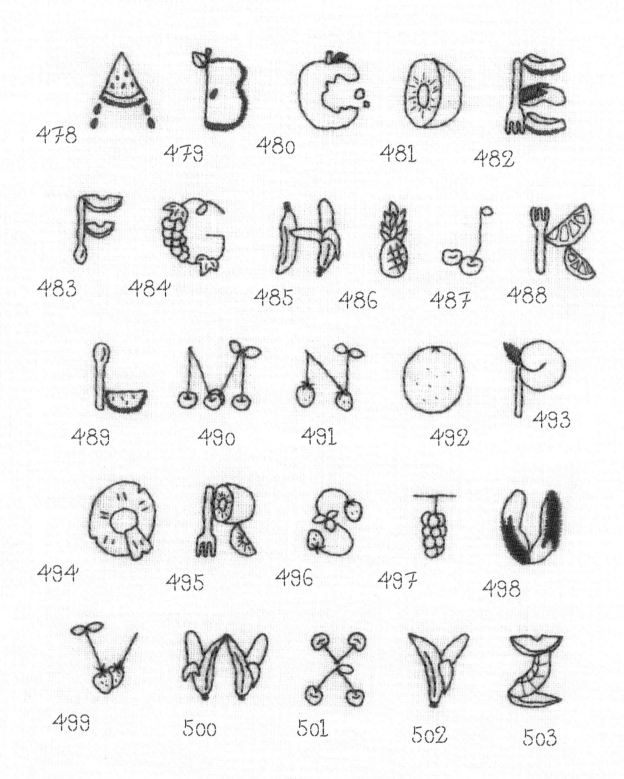

478 479 480 481 482

483 484 485 486 487 488

489 490 491 492 493

494 495 496 497 498

499 500 501 502 503

Letters & Numbers

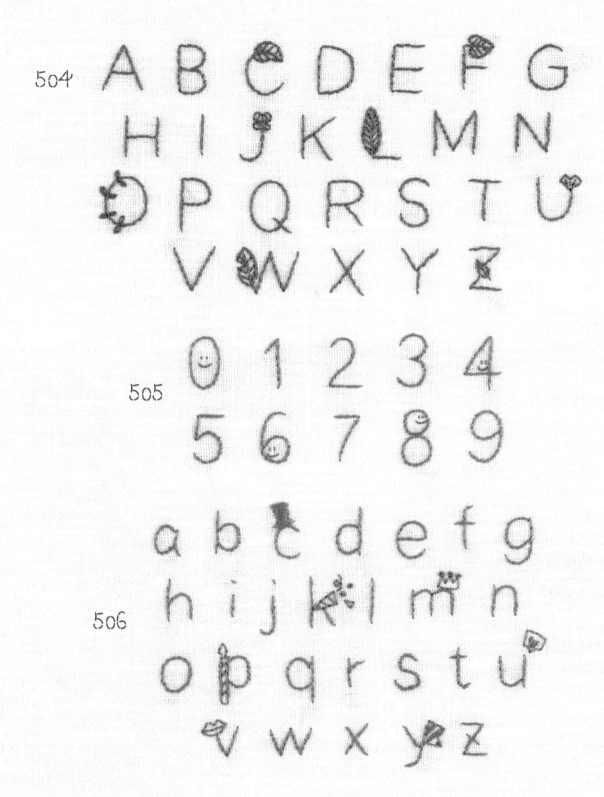

504

A B C D E F G
H I J K L M N
O P Q R S T U
V W X Y Z

505

0 1 2 3 4
5 6 7 8 9

506

a b c d e f g
h i j k l m n
o p q r s t u
v w x y z

Instructions: Pages 120–121

Design & Embroidery: Kumamori

Childhood Favorites

507

508

509

510

511

512

513

514

515

516

517

518

519

520

521

522

Instructions: Pages 122–123
Design & Embroidery: meiP

People & Things

523

524

525

526

527

528

529

530

531

532

533

534

Instructions: Pages 124–127

Design & Embroidery: mona.yu

535

536

537

538

540

539

541

542

543

544

545

546

547

548

549

550

Use the embroidery
motifs to personalize
- pouches,
- t-shirts,
- tote bags,
- linens, and more!

inspiration gallery

254

Page 88

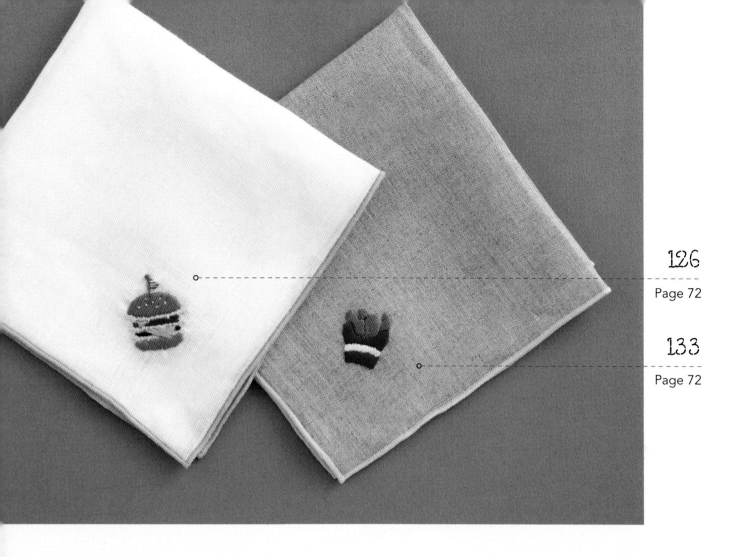

126

Page 72

133

Page 72

POOL

27

Page 58

523

546

459
452
467
476

484
492
481

tools & materials

A. Linen fabric: All of the embroidery in this book was done on linen fabric.

B. No. 25 embroidery floss: This embroidery floss is composed of six thin strands that are loosely twisted together. Separate the strands and use the number noted in the embroidery instructions. Three different brands of embroidery floss were used for the designs in this book (DMC, Olympus, and Cosmo).

C. Embroidery needles: Designed specifically for embroidery, these needles feature a longer eye, allowing for easy threading. Select your needle size based on the number of strands of thread used.

D. Thread snips: Use to cut embroidery floss.

E. Embroidery hoop: Use an embroidery hoop to hold the fabric taut while stitching.

F. Carbon chalk paper: Use to transfer the embroidery designs onto fabric. Refer to page 48 for instructions on transferring the designs.

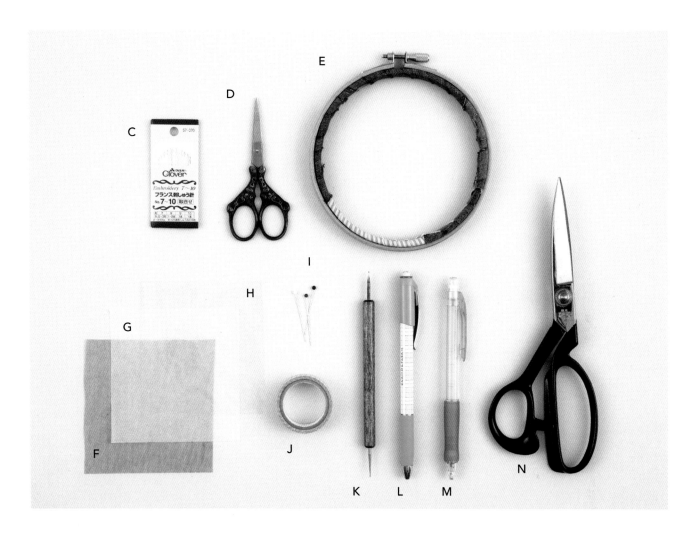

G. Tracing paper: Use to copy the embroidery designs from the book.

H. Cellophane: Use in conjunction with tracing paper and carbon chalk paper to transfer the embroidery designs onto fabric. The cellophane is optional, but will protect the copied design from smudging and will allow for reuse in the future.

I. Pins: Use to hold the copied design in place when transferring it onto the fabric.

J. Masking tape: Use to hold the tracing paper in place when copying the embroidery designs from the book.

K. Stylus: Use to trace the embroidery design during the transfer process. You can also use an empty ballpoint pen.

L. Chalk pen: Use an erasable chalk pen to hand draw designs or fill in areas of the embroidery design that did not transfer completely.

M. Mechanical pencil: Use to copy the embroidery designs onto tracing paper.

N. Fabric scissors: Use to cut fabric.

getting started

HOW TO TRANSFER THE DESIGNS

1. Layer a sheet of tracing paper on top of the embroidery design you wish to transfer from the book. Use a piece of masking tape to hold the paper in place. Trace with a mechanical pencil to copy the design onto the tracing paper.

2. Insert a sheet of carbon chalk paper between the fabric and the tracing paper with the chalk side facing down. Layer a sheet of cellophane on top of the tracing paper. Use a stylus or an empty ballpoint pen to trace over the design again.

3. The pressure from the stylus will transfer the embroidery design onto the fabric. Use a chalk pen to fill in any incomplete lines if necessary.

HOW TO SEPARATE THE EMBROIDERY FLOSS

1. Even if you plan to use all six strands of embroidery floss, it's a good idea to separate the strands prior to stitching in order to help prevent tangles. Start by folding the embroidery floss in half and use the tip of the needle to pull out one strand.

2. Separate the desired number of strands, then recombine them prior to threading the needle.

HOW TO THREAD THE NEEDLE

1. Fold the end of the embroidery floss and insert the needle. Pull the needle upward to form a crease in the floss.

2. Insert the folded end of the floss through the eye of the needle.

3. Draw the folded embroidery floss through the eye of the needle.

HOW TO START & FINISH STITCHING

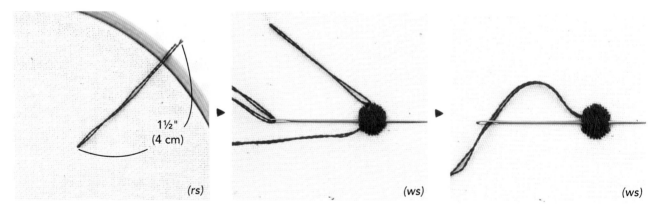

(rs)   (ws)   (ws)

1½" (4 cm)

1. Use the following method to start stitching without tying a knot: Insert the needle through the fabric from the right side of the work, a few inches away from the embroidery design. Leave a 1½" (4 cm) long thread tail, then draw the needle out along the embroidery design.

2. Stitch the embroidery design as noted in the individual instructions. To finish the thread, pass the needle under the stitches on the wrong side of the work a few times, and then trim the excess floss.

3. Rethread the needle with the 1½" (4 cm) long thread tail from step 1. Use the same technique to pass the needle under the stitches on the wrong side, and then trim.

basic stitches

STRAIGHT STITCH

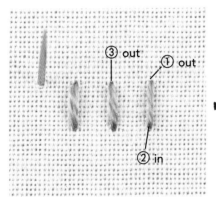 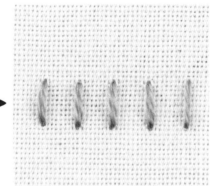 

1. Draw the needle out from the wrong side of the fabric at ①. Make a straight line and insert the needle back into the fabric at ②. Draw the needle out again at ③ to make the next stitch following the same process.

2. Follow this process to make short, straight stitches.

Straight stitch can also be used to fill an area with embroidery.

RUNNING STITCH

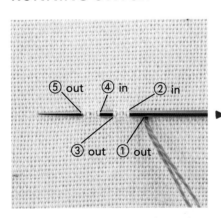 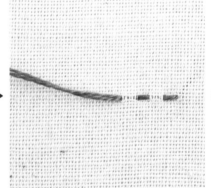 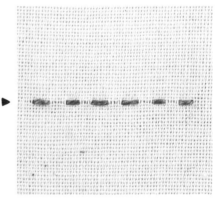

1. Draw the needle out from the wrong side of the fabric at ①. Insert the needle in and out of the fabric at regular intervals.

2. Pull to draw the thread through the fabric.

3. Repeat this process to make several stitches at once.

OUTLINE STITCH

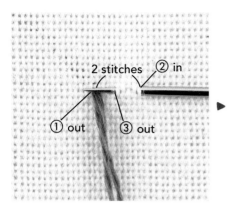

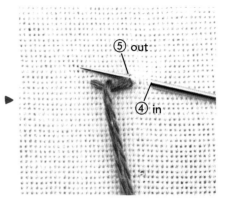

1. Draw the needle out from the wrong side of the fabric at ①. Insert the needle back into the fabric at ②, which is two stitch lengths ahead of ①. Draw the needle out at ③, which is halfway between ① and ②.

2. Pull to draw the thread through the fabric.

3. Insert the needle back through the fabric at ④, which is two stitch lengths ahead of ③. Draw the needle out again at ⑤, which is the same hole as ②.

4. Pull to draw the thread through the fabric.

5. Repeat this process to continue stitching in a line, working from left to right.

Outline stitch can also be used to fill an area with embroidery.

BACKSTITCH

1. Draw the needle out from the wrong side of the fabric at ①, which is one stitch length ahead of the starting point of the design. Insert the needle back through the fabric at ②, which is the starting point. Draw it out again at ③, which is two stitch lengths ahead.

2. Pull to draw the thread through the fabric.

3. Insert the needle back through the fabric at ④, which is the same hole as ①. Draw the needle out again at ⑤, which is two stitch lengths ahead.

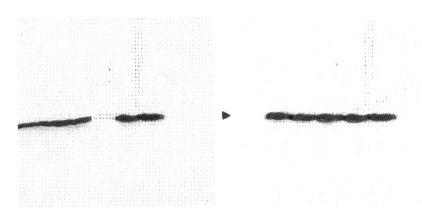

4. Pull to draw the thread through fabric.

5. Repeat this process to continue stitching in a line, working from right to left.

CHAIN STITCH

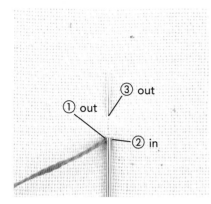

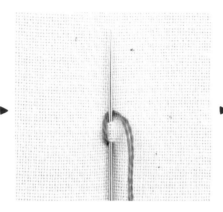

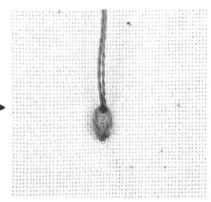

1. Draw the needle out from the wrong side of the fabric at ①. Insert the needle back through the same hole at ②, and then draw it out at ③.

2. Wrap the embroidery floss around the needle.

3. Pull to draw the thread though the fabric, tightening the loop made by the stitches.

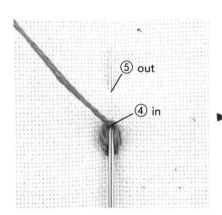

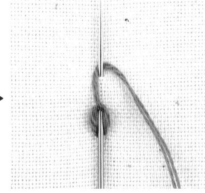

4. Insert the needle back through the fabric at ④, which is the same hole as ③. Draw the needle out again at ⑤.

5. Wrap the embroidery floss around the needle.

6. Pull to draw the thread though the fabric, tightening the loop. Repeat this process to make additional chain stitches.

FRENCH KNOT (WRAP TWICE)

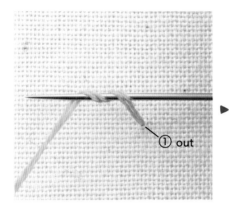

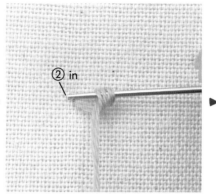

1. Draw the needle out from the wrong side of the fabric at ①. Wrap the embroidery floss around the needle twice (or as many times as noted in the individual instructions).

2. Insert the needle back through the fabric at ②, which is the same hole as ①, keeping the thread wrapped around the needle. Use your finger to help hold the wraps in place if necessary.

3. Pull the thread through the fabric, tightening the knot.

SATIN STITCH

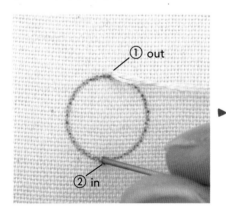

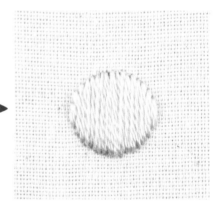

1. Draw the needle out from the wrong side of the fabric at ①, which is positioned at the top center of the design. Insert the needle back through the fabric at ②, which is directly beneath ①.

2. Continue making long, straight stitches to fill the left half of the design. Make sure the stitches are parallel. After completing the left half of the design, return to the top center.

3. Follow the same process to stitch the right half of the design.

LAZY DAISY STITCH

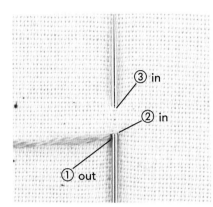

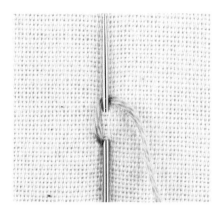

1. Draw the needle out from the wrong side of the fabric at ①. Insert the needle back into the fabric at ②, which is the same hole as ①, and then draw it out again at ③.

2. Wrap the thread around the needle.

3. Pull to draw the thread through the fabric, tightening the loop. This is the same process as making a chain stitch.

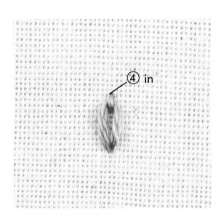

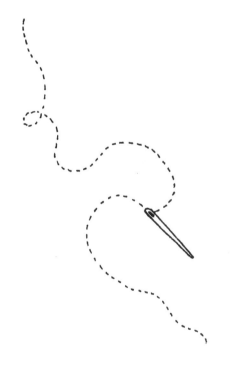

4. Insert the needle back through the fabric at ④, making a small straight stitch to secure the loop.

Assorted Patterns

Photo: page 6

- The numbers represent the color numbers for DMC No. 25 embroidery floss
- The numbers in ◯ represent the number of strands of thread
- Wrap French knots twice, unless otherwise noted

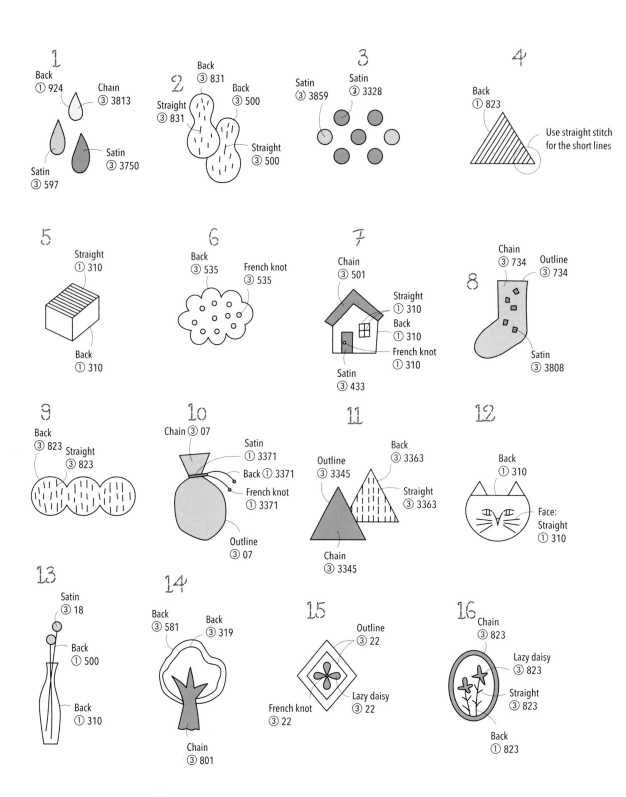

1
Back ① 924
Chain ③ 3813
Satin ③ 3750
Satin ③ 597

2
Back ③ 831
Straight ③ 831
Back ③ 500
Straight ③ 500

3
Satin ③ 3859
Satin ③ 3328

4
Back ① 823
Use straight stitch for the short lines

5
Straight ① 310
Back ① 310

6
Back ③ 535
French knot ③ 535

7
Chain ③ 501
Straight ① 310
Back ① 310
French knot ① 310
Satin ③ 433

8
Chain ③ 734
Outline ③ 734
Satin ③ 3808

9
Back ③ 823
Straight ③ 823

10
Chain ③ 07
Satin ① 3371
Back ① 3371
French knot ① 3371
Outline ③ 07

11
Outline ③ 3345
Back ③ 3363
Straight ③ 3363
Chain ③ 3345

12
Back ① 310
Face: Straight ① 310

13
Satin ③ 18
Back ① 500
Back ① 310

14
Back ③ 581
Back ③ 319
Chain ③ 801

15
Outline ③ 22
Lazy daisy ③ 22
French knot ③ 22

16
Chain ③ 823
Lazy daisy ③ 823
Straight ③ 823
Back ① 823

1

2

3

4

5

6

7

8

9

10

11

12

13

14

15

16

Simple Flowers

Photo: page 7

■ The numbers represent the color numbers for DMC No. 25 embroidery floss
■ The numbers in ◯ represent the number of strands of thread
■ Wrap French knots twice, unless otherwise noted

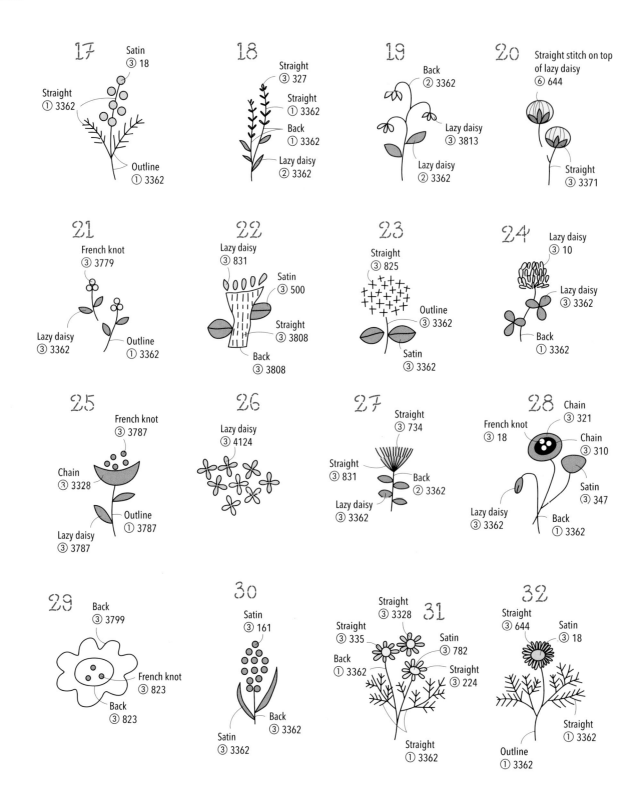

17
Satin ③ 18
Straight ① 3362
Outline ① 3362

18
Straight ③ 327
Straight ① 3362
Back ① 3362
Lazy daisy ② 3362

19
Back ② 3362
Lazy daisy ③ 3813
Lazy daisy ② 3362

20
Straight stitch on top of lazy daisy ⑥ 644
Straight ③ 3371

21
French knot ③ 3779
Lazy daisy ③ 3362
Outline ① 3362

22
Lazy daisy ③ 831
Satin ③ 500
Straight ③ 3808
Back ③ 3808

23
Straight ③ 825
Outline ③ 3362
Satin ③ 3362

24
Lazy daisy ③ 10
Lazy daisy ③ 3362
Back ① 3362

25
French knot ③ 3787
Chain ③ 3328
Outline ① 3787
Lazy daisy ③ 3787

26
Lazy daisy ③ 4124

27
Straight ③ 734
Straight ③ 831
Back ② 3362
Lazy daisy ③ 3362

28
Chain ③ 321
French knot ③ 18
Chain ③ 310
Satin ③ 347
Lazy daisy ③ 3362
Back ① 3362

29
Back ③ 3799
French knot ③ 823
Back ③ 823

30
Satin ③ 161
Back ③ 3362
Satin ③ 3362

31
Straight ③ 3328
Straight ③ 335
Back ① 3362
Satin ③ 782
Straight ③ 224
Straight ① 3362

32
Straight ③ 644
Satin ③ 18
Straight ① 3362
Outline ① 3362

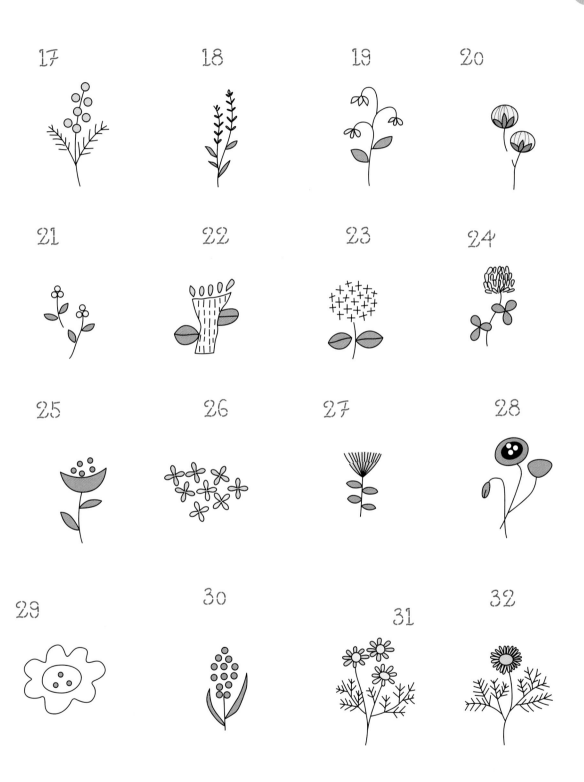

17   18   19   20

21   22   23   24

25   26   27   28

29   30   31   32

Folk Art Flowers

Photo: page 8

- The numbers represent the color numbers for DMC No. 25 embroidery floss
- The numbers in ○ represent the number of strands of thread
- Wrap French knots twice, unless otherwise noted

33
Satin ③ 3362
Satin ③ 3777
French knot ③ 3865

34
Satin ③ 829
French knot ③ 3033
Straight ③ 3052
Satin ③ 3052

35
Satin ③ 3865
Straight ② 3362
Outline ② 3362
Satin ③ 3362

36
French knot ③ 3865
Satin ③ 435
Satin ③ 3033
Satin ③ 3052
Outline ② 3862

37
Satin ③ 924
Straight ③ 3052
Satin ③ 3052

38
Satin ③ 3726
Outline ③ 3347
Satin ③ 3347

39
Satin ③ 3045
French knot ③ 3045
Outline ③ 3362
Satin ③ 3362

40
Satin ③ 3740
Straight ② 3862
Satin ③ 372
Outline ③ 372

41
Satin ③ 3865
Outline ② 3362
Satin ③ 3362

42
Satin ③ 924
Satin ③ 3865

43
Satin ③ 3064
French knot ③ 3033
Straight ③ 3347
Outline ② 3862

44
Satin ③ 647
Satin ③ 829
Satin ③ 3345
Outline ② 938

45
Satin ③ 223
Straight ② 640
Outline ② 3052
Satin ③ 3052

46
Satin ③ 434
Satin ③ 3865
French knot ③ 3865
Satin ③ 3345

47
Satin ③ 3858
Satin ③ 372
Outline ② 372

48
French knot ③ 833
Satin ③ 3033
Outline ② 3362
Straight ③ 3362

33 34 35 36

37 38 39 40

41 42 43 44

45 46 47 48

Folk Art Flowers

Photo: page 9

■ The numbers represent the color numbers for DMC No. 25 embroidery floss
■ The numbers in ◯ represent the number of strands of thread
■ Wrap French knots twice, unless otherwise noted

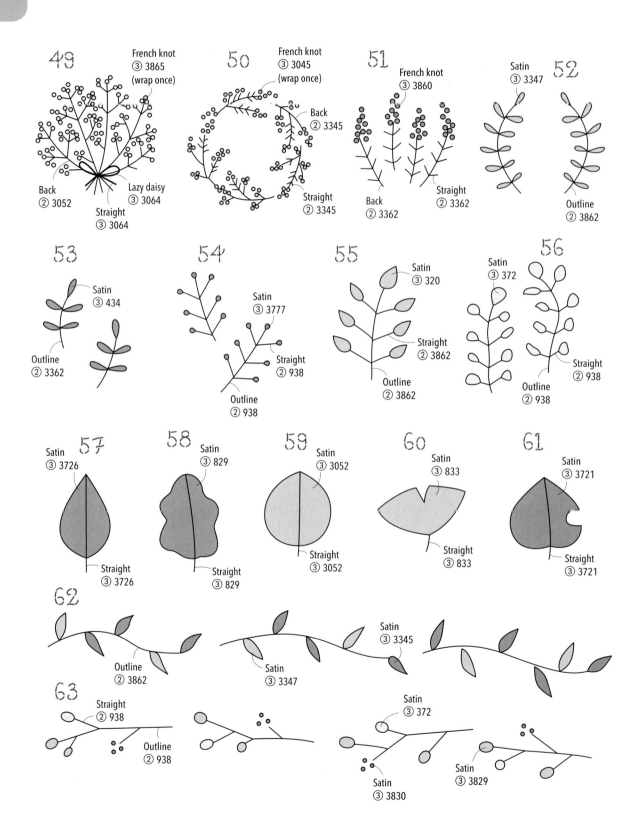

49 — French knot ③ 3865 (wrap once), Back ② 3052, Straight ③ 3064, Lazy daisy ③ 3064

50 — French knot ③ 3045 (wrap once), Back ② 3345, Straight ② 3345

51 — French knot ③ 3860, Back ② 3362, Straight ② 3362

52 — Satin ③ 3347, Outline ② 3862

53 — Satin ③ 434, Outline ② 3362

54 — Satin ③ 3777, Straight ② 938, Outline ② 938

55 — Satin ③ 320, Straight ② 3862, Outline ② 3862

56 — Satin ③ 372, Straight ② 938, Outline ② 938

57 — Satin ③ 3726, Straight ③ 3726

58 — Satin ③ 829, Straight ③ 829

59 — Satin ③ 3052, Straight ③ 3052

60 — Satin ③ 833, Straight ③ 833

61 — Satin ③ 3721, Straight ③ 3721

62 — Outline ② 3862, Satin ③ 3347, Satin ③ 3345

63 — Straight ② 938, Outline ② 938, Satin ③ 372, Satin ③ 3830, Satin ③ 3829

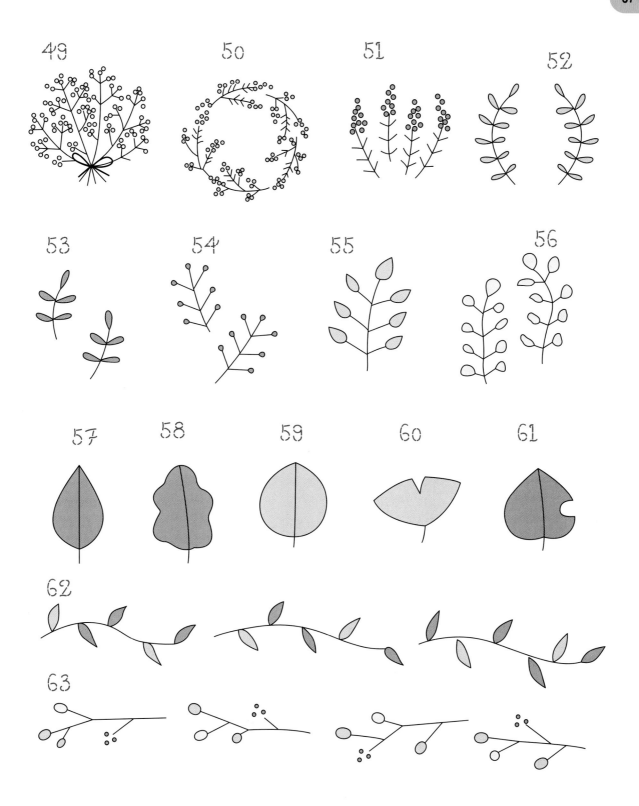

49 50 51 52

53 54 55 56

57 58 59 60 61

62

63

Fairytale Flowers

Photo: page 10

- The numbers represent the color numbers for Olympus No. 25 embroidery floss
- The numbers in ○ represent the number of strands of thread
- Wrap French knots twice, unless otherwise noted

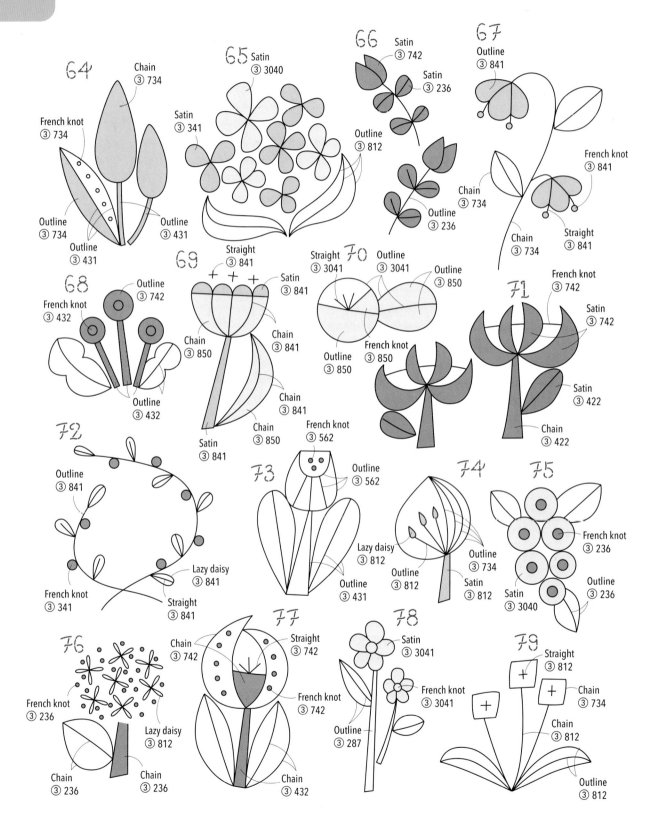

64
Chain ③ 734
French knot ③ 734
Outline ③ 734
Outline ③ 431
Outline ③ 431

65
Satin ③ 3040
Satin ③ 341

66
Satin ③ 742
Satin ③ 236
Outline ③ 812
Outline ③ 236

67
Outline ③ 841
French knot ③ 841
Chain ③ 734
Chain ③ 734
Straight ③ 841

68
Outline ③ 742
French knot ③ 432
Outline ③ 432

69
Straight ③ 841
Satin ③ 841
Chain ③ 850
Chain ③ 841
Chain ③ 841
Satin ③ 841
Chain ③ 850

70
Straight ③ 3041
Outline ③ 3041
Outline ③ 850
French knot ③ 850
Outline ③ 850

71
French knot ③ 742
Satin ③ 742
Satin ③ 422
Chain ③ 422

72
Outline ③ 841
French knot ③ 341
Lazy daisy ③ 841
Straight ③ 841

73
French knot ③ 562
Outline ③ 562
Lazy daisy ③ 812
Outline ③ 431

74
Outline ③ 734
Outline ③ 812
Satin ③ 812

75
French knot ③ 236
Satin ③ 3040
Outline ③ 236

76
French knot ③ 236
Lazy daisy ③ 812
Chain ③ 236
Chain ③ 236

77
Chain ③ 742
Straight ③ 742
French knot ③ 742
Chain ③ 432

78
Satin ③ 3041
French knot ③ 3041
Outline ③ 287

79
Straight ③ 812
Chain ③ 734
Chain ③ 812
Outline ③ 812

64

65

66

67

68

69 + + +

70

71

72

73

74

75

76

77

78

79

Fairytale Flowers

Photo: page 11

- The numbers represent the color numbers for Olympus No. 25 embroidery floss
- The numbers in ◯ represent the number of strands of thread
- Wrap French knots twice, unless otherwise noted

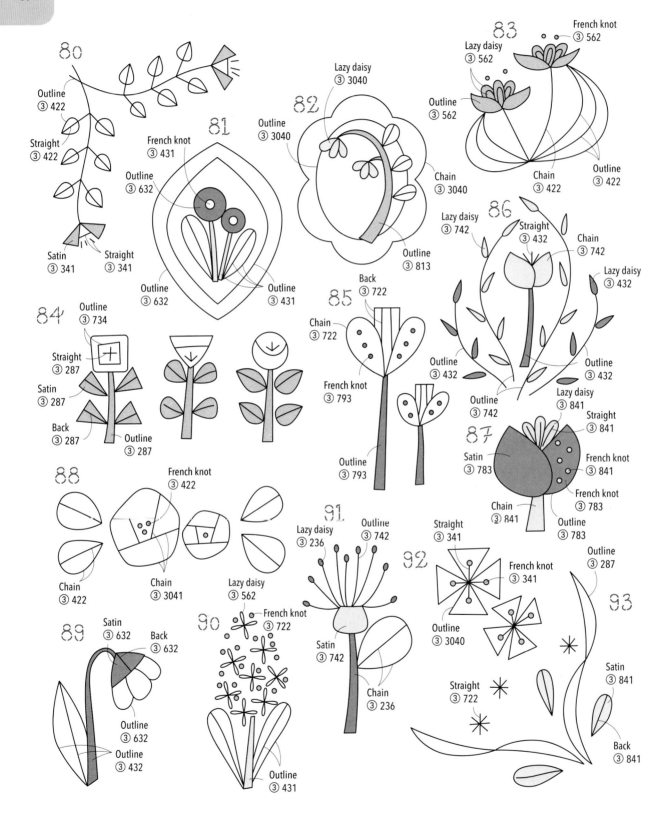

80
Outline ③ 422
Straight ③ 422
Satin ③ 341
Straight ③ 341

81
French knot ③ 431
Outline ③ 632
Outline ③ 632
Outline ③ 431

82
Lazy daisy ③ 3040
Outline ③ 3040
Chain ③ 3040
Outline ③ 813

83
French knot ③ 562
Lazy daisy ③ 562
Outline ③ 562
Chain ③ 422
Outline ③ 422

84
Outline ③ 734
Straight ③ 287
Satin ③ 287
Back ③ 287
Outline ③ 287

85
Back ③ 722
Chain ③ 722
French knot ③ 793
Outline ③ 793

86
Lazy daisy ③ 742
Straight ③ 432
Chain ③ 742
Lazy daisy ③ 432
Outline ③ 432
Outline ③ 742
Lazy daisy ③ 841
Straight ③ 841

87
Satin ③ 783
French knot ③ 841
French knot ③ 783
Chain ③ 841
Outline ③ 783

88
French knot ③ 422
Chain ③ 422
Chain ③ 3041
Lazy daisy ③ 562

89
Satin ③ 632
Back ③ 632
Outline ③ 632
Outline ③ 432

90
French knot ③ 722
Outline ③ 431

91
Lazy daisy ③ 236
Outline ③ 742
Satin ③ 742
Chain ③ 236

92
Straight ③ 341
French knot ③ 341
Outline ③ 3040
Straight ③ 722

93
Outline ③ 287
Satin ③ 841
Back ③ 841

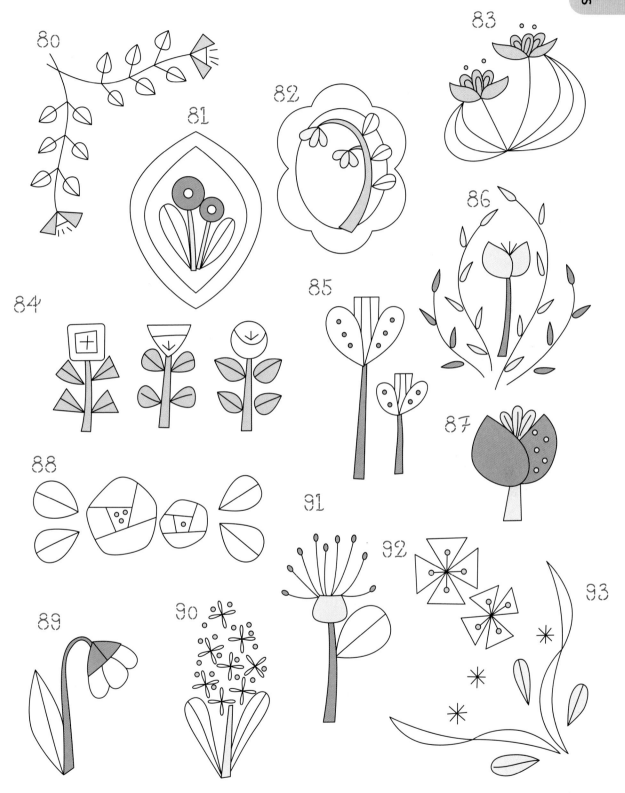

Breakfast Foods

Photo: page 12

- The numbers represent the color numbers for DMC No. 25 embroidery floss
- The numbers in ◯ represent the number of strands of thread
- Wrap French knots twice, unless otherwise noted

94
Chain ③ 938
Outline ③ 612
Chain ③ 612

95
Chain ③ 801
Straight ③ 422
Chain ③ 435

96
Outline ③ 435
Chain ③ 422
Chain ③ ECRU

97
Back ① 310

98
Outline ① 938
French knot ③ ECRU
Chain ③ 435
Back ① 938

99
Satin ③ 3371

100
Chain ③ 938
Outline ③ 676
Chain ③ 676

101
Back ① 310

102
Chain ③ 3371
Outline ③ 3371
Outline ③ 422
Chain ③ 422

103
Back ① 310

104
Back ① 310
Chain ③ 676
Straight ① 3818
Chain ③ ECRU

105
Outline ③ 310
Satin ③ 22
Chain ③ BLANC

106
Chain ③ 435
Satin ③ 3047
Chain ③ 676
Chain ③ 422

107
French knot ③ ECRU
Outline ③ 3799
Straight ③ 3799
Satin ③ 3799

108
Satin ③ 938
Chain ③ 612

109
Chain ③ 400
Outline ③ 03
Chain ③ 03

94

95

96

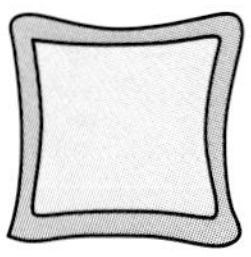

97

98

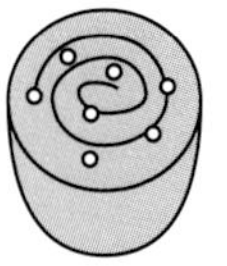

99

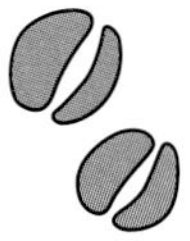

100

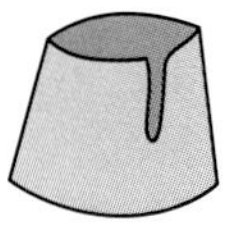

101

102

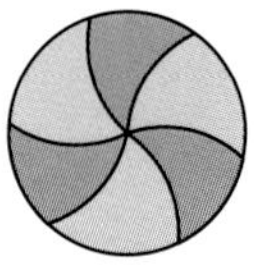

103

104

105

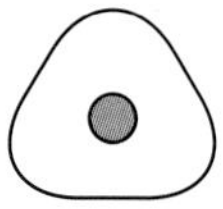

106

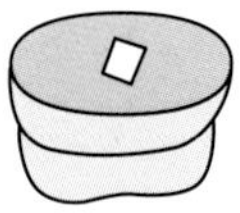

107

108

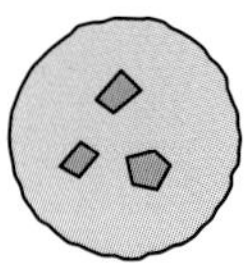

109

Fruits & Vegetables

Photo: page 13

- The numbers represent the color numbers for DMC No. 25 embroidery floss
- The numbers in ◯ represent the number of strands of thread
- Wrap French knots twice, unless otherwise noted

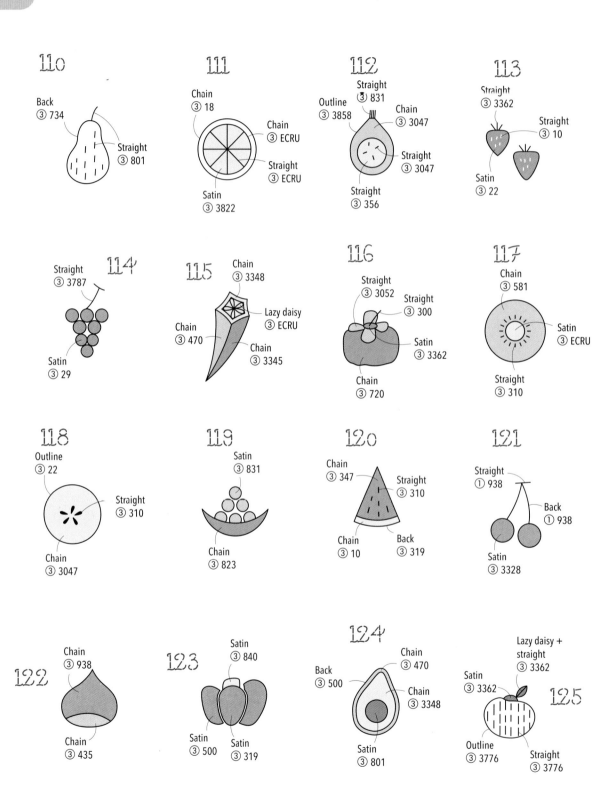

110
Back ③ 734
Straight ③ 801

111
Chain ③ 18
Chain ③ ECRU
Straight ③ ECRU
Satin ③ 3822

112
Straight ③ 831
Outline ③ 3858
Chain ③ 3047
Straight ③ 3047
Straight ③ 356

113
Straight ③ 3362
Straight ③ 10
Satin ③ 22

114
Straight ③ 3787
Satin ③ 29

115
Chain ③ 3348
Lazy daisy ③ ECRU
Chain ③ 470
Chain ③ 3345

116
Straight ③ 3052
Straight ③ 300
Satin ③ 3362
Chain ③ 720

117
Chain ③ 581
Satin ③ ECRU
Straight ③ 310

118
Outline ③ 22
Straight ③ 310
Chain ③ 3047

119
Satin ③ 831
Chain ③ 823

120
Chain ③ 347
Straight ③ 310
Chain ③ 10
Back ③ 319

121
Straight ① 938
Back ① 938
Satin ③ 3328

122
Chain ③ 938
Chain ③ 435

123
Satin ③ 840
Satin ③ 500
Satin ③ 319

124
Back ③ 500
Chain ③ 470
Chain ③ 3348
Satin ③ 801

125
Lazy daisy + straight ③ 3362
Satin ③ 3362
Outline ③ 3776
Straight ③ 3776

110

111

112

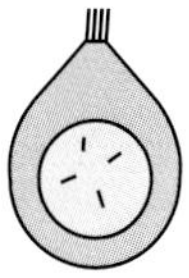

113

114

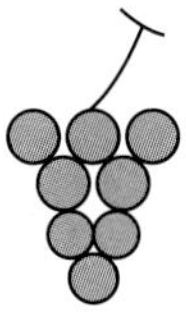

115

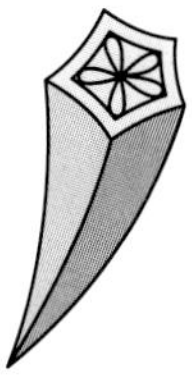

116

117

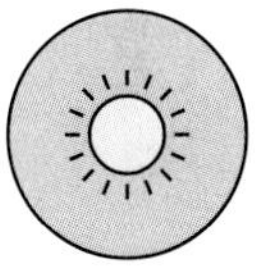

118

119

120

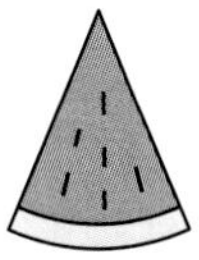

121

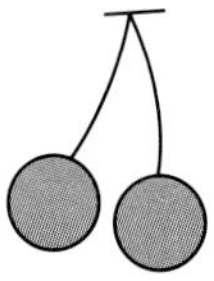

122

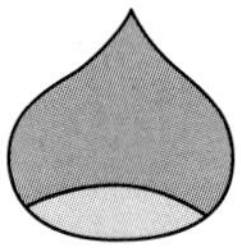

123

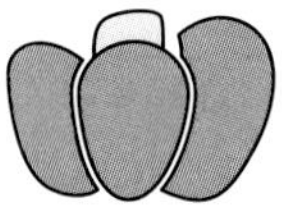

124

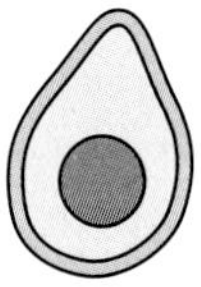

125

Favorite Foods

Photo: page 14

- The numbers represent the color numbers for Olympus No. 25 embroidery floss
- The numbers in ○ represent the number of strands of thread
- Wrap French knots twice, unless otherwise noted

126
French knot ③ 127 (wrap once)
Straight ③ 127
Satin ③ 700
Straight ③ 734
Straight ③ 800
Satin ③ 712
Satin ③ 190
Satin ③ 228
Satin ③ 532
Satin ③ 778

127
Satin ③ 700
Satin ③ 712
Satin ③ 532

128
Satin ③ 190
Satin ③ 712
Satin ③ 900
Satin ③ 190
Satin ③ 551
Lazy daisy ③ 276 Stitch on top of satin ③ 551

129
French knot ③ 800
Satin ③ 700
Satin ③ 800

130
Satin ③ 733
Satin ③ 532
Satin ③ 190

131
Satin ③ 119
Satin ③ 734
Satin ③ 228
Satin ③ 850
Satin ③ 190
Satin ③ 734

132
Satin ③ 735
Satin + French knot ③ 785 (wrap once)

133
Satin ③ 712
Satin ③ 850
Satin ③ 190

134
Satin ③ 170
Satin ③ 119
Satin ③ 734

135
Satin ③ 546
Satin ③ 700
Straight ③ 546
Straight ③ 700
Satin ③ 546
Satin ③ 700

136
Outline ③ 800
Satin ③ 800
Satin ③ 739
Satin ③ 700
Satin ③ 800

137
Straight ③ 484
Satin ③ 785
Satin ③ 231
Straight ③ 484
Satin ③ 785
Satin ③ 551
Satin ③ 231
Satin ③ 532
Straight ③ 484
Outline ③ 484

138
Straight ③ 734
Straight ③ 540
Satin ③ 778
Satin ③ 735
Straight ③ 231
Satin ③ 734

139
Outline ③ 1041 Alternate ③ 733 colors
Satin ③ 1041
Satin ③ 900
Straight ③ 733
Satin ③ 712
Back ③ 145
Back ③ 119
Satin ③ 735
Satin ③ 800
Satin ③ 521
Outline ③ 800

140
Straight ③ 540
Satin ③ 734

141
Satin ③ 712
Satin ③ 778
Satin ③ 484
Satin ③ 734
Straight ③ 231
Straight ③ 735

126

127

128

129

130

131

132

133

134

135

136

137

138

139

140

141

Sweets & Treats

Photo: page 15

- The numbers represent the color numbers for Olympus No. 25 embroidery floss
- The numbers in ◯ represent the number of strands of thread
- Wrap French knots twice, unless otherwise noted

142
Satin ③ 192
Satin ③ 210
Satin ③ 800
Satin ③ 521
French knot ③ 192 (wrap once)

143
Outline ③ 731 ③ 800 } Alternate colors
Satin ③ 712
Straight ③ 712
Satin ③ 712

144
French knot ③ 521 ③ 1041 ③ 219 (wrap once)
Satin ③ 778
Satin ③ 734
Straight ③ 731

145
Satin ③ 521
Satin ③ 800
Straight ③ 735
Satin ③ 712
Satin ③ 551
Back ③ 778
Satin ③ 103

146
Satin ③ 712
Satin ③ 800
Satin ③ 735
Satin ③ 734

147
Satin ③ 192
Satin ③ 778
Satin ③ 734
Back ③ 383
French knot ③ 778

148
Satin ③ 700
Satin ③ 190
Back ③ 700
French knot ③ 800 (wrap once)
Satin ③ 228
French knot ③ 358 (wrap once)
Satin ③ 540
Satin ③ 778
Satin ③ 532
Satin ③ 800
Satin ③ 483
Satin ③ 521

149
Satin ③ 735
Satin ③ 800

150
Back ③ 190
Satin ③ 1041
Satin ③ 190
Straight ③ 383
Satin ③ 778
Back ③ 735
Satin ③ 735
Stitch one grid at a time, changing direction

151
Satin ③ 712
Satin ③ 521
Satin ③ 800

152
Satin ③ 276
Satin ③ 190
Satin ③ 655
Satin ③ 778
Satin ③ 733

153
Satin ③ 190
Satin ③ 800
Satin ③ 735
Satin ③ 1041
Satin ③ 228
Satin ③ 190
Satin ③ 778
Satin ③ 733
Satin ③ 1041
Outline ③ 370
Satin ③ 800
Satin ③ 190
Satin ③ 735
Satin ③ 370A

154
French knot ③ 738
Satin ③ 811
Outline ③ 190
Satin ③ 503
Satin ③ 542
Satin ③ 738
Satin ③ 190
Satin ③ 739
Satin ③ 811
Satin ③ 778
Satin ③ 800
Satin ③ 228
Satin ③ 117

155
Satin ③ 503
Satin ③ 735
Satin ③ 551

156
Satin ③ 190
Satin ③ 228
Satin ③ 1041
Satin ③ 358
Satin ③ 735
Satin ③ 800

157
Satin ③ 800
Satin ③ 739
Satin ③ 190
Satin ③ 190
Satin ③ 735
Satin ③ 1041

142

143

144

145

146

147

148

149

150

151

152

153

154

155

156

157

Zodiac Animals

Photo: page 16

- The numbers represent the color numbers for DMC No. 25 embroidery floss
- The numbers in ○ represent the number of strands of thread
- Wrap French knots twice, unless otherwise noted

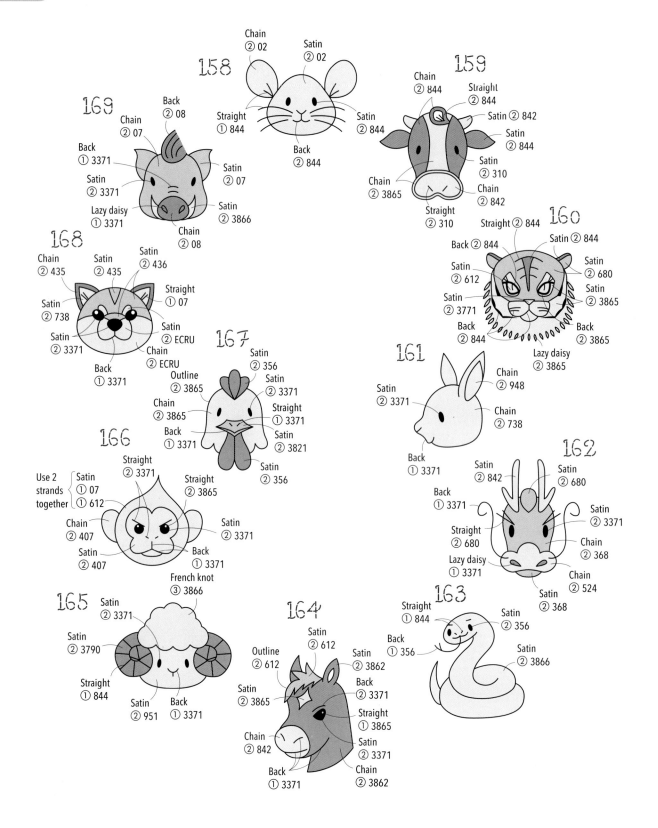

158
159
169
168
160
167
166
161
162
165
164
163

Dogs & Cats

Photo: page 17

- The numbers represent the color numbers for DMC No. 25 embroidery floss
- The numbers in ○ represent the number of strands of thread
- Wrap French knots twice, unless otherwise noted
- Satin ② 3371 for the eyes and straight ① BLANC for the eye highlights, unless otherwise noted

170

171

172

173

176

174

175

177

178

179

180

181

182

183

184

185

Favorite Animals

Photo: page 18

- The numbers represent the color numbers for DMC No. 25 embroidery floss
- The numbers in ◯ represent the number of strands of thread
- Wrap French knots twice, unless otherwise noted

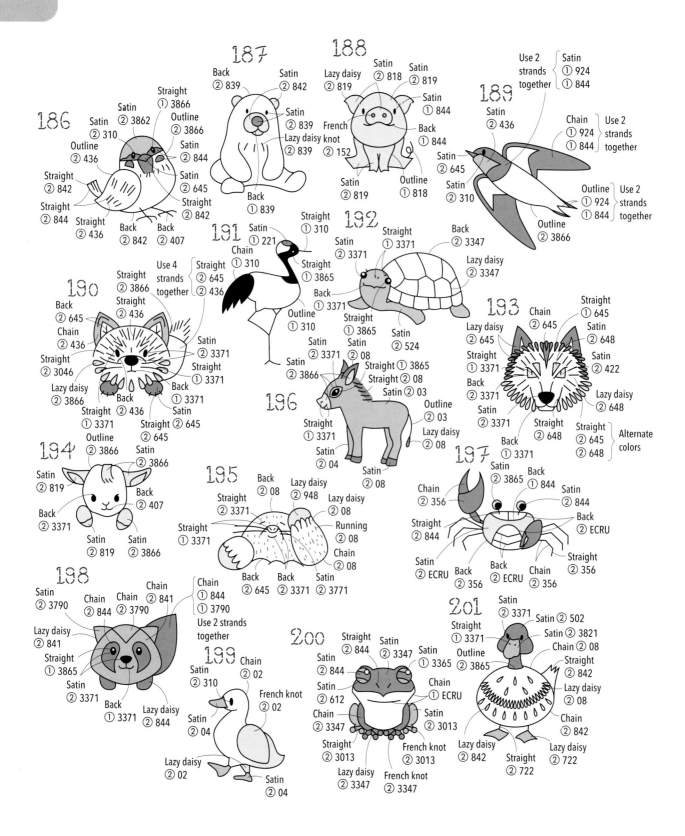

186
Satin ② 3862
Satin ② 310
Outline ② 436
Straight ② 842
Straight ② 844
Satin ① 3866
Straight ② 436
Back ② 842
Back ② 407

187
Back ② 839
Satin ② 842
Outline ② 3866
Satin ② 839
Satin ② 844
Satin ② 645
Straight ② 842
Back ① 839

188
Lazy daisy ② 819
Satin ② 818
Satin ② 819
Satin ① 844
Back ① 844
French ① 152
Satin ② 819
Outline ① 818

189
Use 2 strands together { Satin ① 924 / ① 844 }
Satin ② 436
Chain ① 924 / ① 844 Use 2 strands together
Satin ② 645
Satin ② 310
Outline ① 924 / ① 844 Use 2 strands together
Outline ② 3866

190
Back ② 645
Chain ② 436
Straight ② 3046
Lazy daisy ② 3866
Straight ① 3371
Back ② 436
Straight ② 3866
Straight ② 436
Use 4 strands together { Straight ② 645 / ② 436 }
Satin ② 3371
Straight ① 3371
Back ① 3371
Satin ② 645

191
Satin ① 221
Chain ① 310
Straight ① 3865
Back ① 3371
Outline ① 310
Satin ② 3371
Satin ② 3866

192
Straight ① 310
Satin ② 3371
Straight ① 3371
Back ② 3347
Lazy daisy ② 3347
Straight ① 3865
Satin ② 08
Straight ① 3865
Satin ② 524

193
Chain ② 645
Straight ① 645
Satin ② 648
Lazy daisy ② 645
Straight ① 3371
Satin ② 422
Back ② 3371
Lazy daisy ② 648
Satin ② 3371
Back ① 3371
Straight ② 648
Straight ② 645 / ② 648 Alternate colors

194
Outline ② 3866
Satin ② 3866
Satin ② 819
Back ② 407
Back ② 3371
Satin ② 819
Satin ② 3866

195
Back ② 08
Lazy daisy ② 948
Straight ② 3371
Lazy daisy ② 08
Running ② 08
Straight ① 3371
Chain ② 08
Back ② 645
Back ② 3371
Satin ② 3771

196
Straight ① 3371
Satin ② 04
Satin ② 3371
Satin ② 08
Straight ① 3865
Straight ② 08
Satin ② 03
Outline ② 03
Lazy daisy ② 08
Satin ② 08

197
Satin ② 3865
Back ① 844
Satin ② 844
Chain ② 356
Straight ② 844
Back ② ECRU
Satin ② ECRU
Back ② 356
Back ② ECRU
Chain ② 356
Straight ② 356

198
Satin ② 3790
Chain ② 844
Chain ② 3790
Chain ② 3790
Chain ② 841
Chain ① 844 / ① 3790 Use 2 strands together
Lazy daisy ② 841
Straight ① 3865
Satin ② 3371
Back ① 3371
Lazy daisy ② 844

199
Satin ② 310
Chain ② 02
French knot ② 02
Satin ② 04
Lazy daisy ② 02
Satin ② 04

200
Straight ② 844
Satin ② 3347
Satin ② 844
Satin ① 3365
Satin ② 612
Chain ① ECRU
Chain ② 3347
Satin ② 3013
Straight ② 3013
Lazy daisy ② 3347
French knot ② 3013
French knot ② 3347

201
Satin ② 3371
Satin ② 502
Straight ① 3371
Satin ② 3821
Outline ② 3865
Chain ② 08
Straight ② 842
Lazy daisy ② 08
Lazy daisy ② 842
Satin ② 842
Lazy daisy ② 722
Straight ② 722

186

187

188

189

190

191

192

193

194

195

196

197

198

199

200

201

Favorite Animals

Photo: page 19

- The numbers represent the color numbers for DMC No. 25 embroidery floss
- The numbers in ◯ represent the number of strands of thread
- Wrap French knots twice, unless otherwise noted
- Satin ② 3371 for the eyes, unless otherwise noted
- Straight ① BLANC for the eye highlights, unless otherwise noted

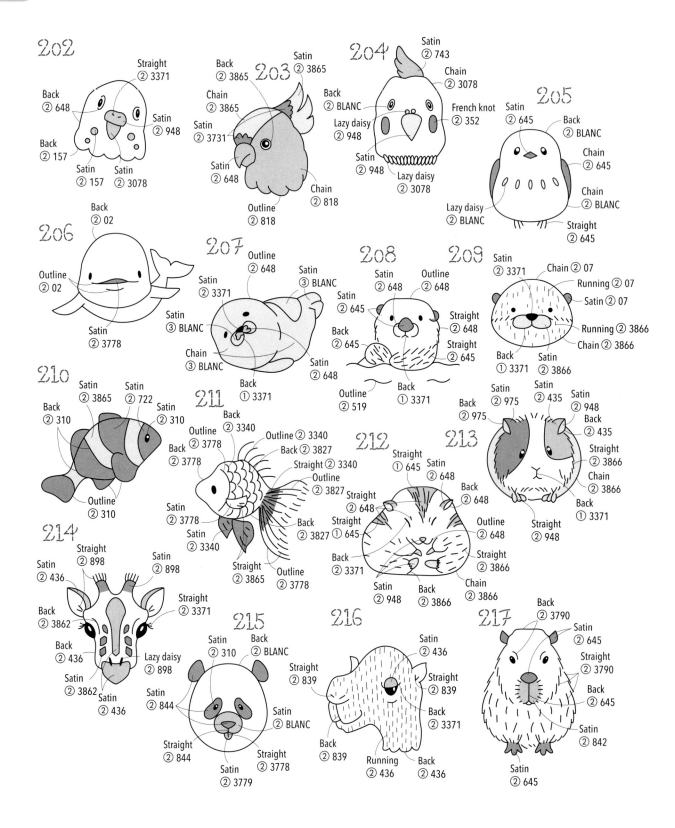

202 203 204 205 206 207 208 209 210 211 212 213 214 215 216 217

Animal Friends

Photo: page 20

■ The numbers represent the color numbers for DMC No. 25 embroidery floss
■ The numbers in ◯ represent the number of strands of thread
■ Wrap French knots twice, unless otherwise noted
■ Straight ① 310 for the eyes, nose, and mouth, unless otherwise noted

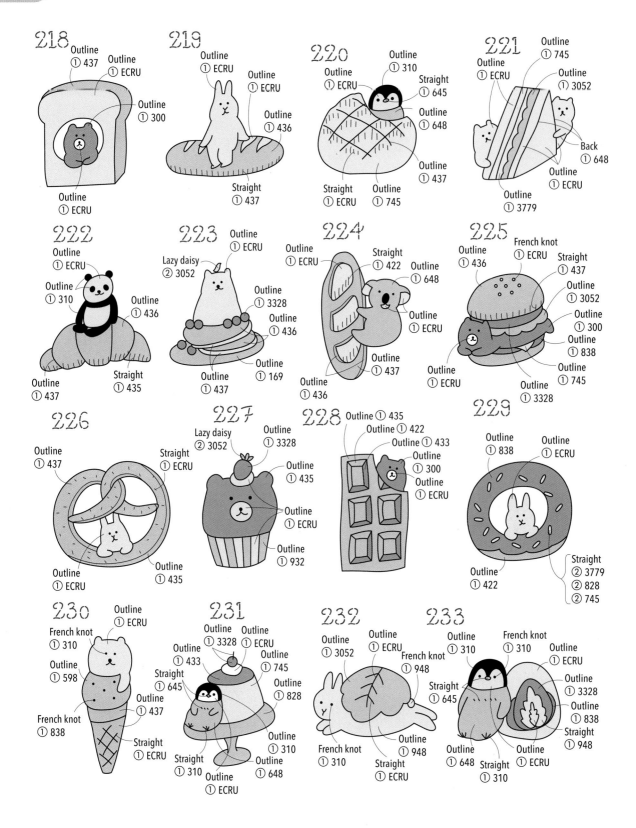

218
Outline ① 437
Outline ① ECRU
Outline ① 300
Outline ① ECRU

219
Outline ① ECRU
Outline ① ECRU
Outline ① 436
Straight ① 437

220
Outline ① 310
Outline ① ECRU
Straight ① 645
Outline ① 648
Outline ① 437
Straight ① ECRU
Outline ① 745

221
Outline ① 745
Outline ① ECRU
Outline ① 3052
Back ① 648
Outline ① ECRU
Outline ① 3779

222
Outline ① ECRU
Outline ① 310
Outline ① 436
Outline ① 437
Straight ① 435

223
Outline ① ECRU
Lazy daisy ② 3052
Outline ① 3328
Outline ① 436
Outline ① 169
Outline ① 437

224
Outline ① ECRU
Straight ① 422
Outline ① 648
Outline ① ECRU
Outline ① 437
Outline ① 436

225
Outline ① 436
French knot ① ECRU
Straight ① 437
Outline ① 3052
Outline ① 300
Outline ① 838
Outline ① 745
Outline ① 3328

226
Outline ① 437
Straight ① ECRU
Outline ① ECRU
Outline ① 435

227
Lazy daisy ② 3052
Outline ① 3328
Outline ① 435
Outline ① ECRU
Outline ① 932

228
Outline ① 435
Outline ① 422
Outline ① 433
Outline ① 300
Outline ① ECRU

229
Outline ① 838
Outline ① ECRU
Outline ① 422
Straight ② 3779
② 828
② 745

230
Outline ① ECRU
French knot ① 310
Outline ① 598
French knot ① 838
Outline ① 437
Straight ① ECRU

231
Outline ① 3328
Outline ① ECRU
Outline ① 433
Outline ① 745
Straight ① 645
Outline ① 828
Outline ① 437
Outline ① 310
Outline ① 648
Straight ① 310
Outline ① ECRU

232
Outline ① 3052
Outline ① ECRU
French knot ① 948
Straight ① 645
French knot ① 310
Outline ① 948
Straight ① ECRU

233
Outline ① 310
French knot ① 310
Outline ① ECRU
Outline ① 3328
Outline ① 838
Straight ① 948
Outline ① 648
Straight ① 310
Outline ① ECRU

218 219 220 221

222 223 224 225

226 227 228 229

230 231 232 233

Animal Friends

Photo: page 21

- The numbers represent the color numbers for DMC No. 25 embroidery floss
- The numbers in ◯ represent the number of strands of thread
- Wrap French knots twice, unless otherwise noted
- Straight ① 310 for the eyes, noses, and mouth, unless otherwise noted

234

235

236

237

238

239

240

241

242

243

244

245

246

247

248

249

Fairytale Animals

Photo: page 22

- The numbers represent the color numbers for DMC No. 25 embroidery floss
- The numbers in ○ represent the number of strands of thread
- Wrap French knots twice, unless otherwise noted
- Straight ① 3781 for the eyes and whiskers, unless otherwise noted
- French knot ① 3781 for the noses, unless otherwise noted

250
Chain ② 3821
Satin ② 729
Outline ② 3781
Satin ② 822
Straight ② 822
Satin ② E677
Straight ② 3781
Satin ② 918
Satin ② 729
Satin ② 3781

251
Running ① E677
Chain ② 3821
Satin ② 3023
Satin ② E677
Satin ② 3023
Chain ② 3053
Straight ② 3781

252
Satin ② 822
Satin ② 502
Chain ② 451
Satin ② E677
Satin ② 3821
Chain ② 758
Satin ② E677

253
Chain ② 3778
Chain ② 502
Outline ② 3781
Satin ② 822
Satin ② E677
Satin ② 3787
Straight ② 3781

254
Chain ② 822
Chain ② 729
Chain ② 918
Chain ② 3768
Lazy daisy ② 918
Satin ② 822
Outline ② 3787
Satin ② E677
Straight ② 3821
Lazy daisy ② 918
Satin ② 3023
Chain ② 610

255
Chain ② 3053
Chain ② 422
Satin ② 3045
Satin ② E677
Outline ② 3781
Straight ② 3781
Straight ② 3781
Satin ② 918
Satin ② 3045

256
Chain ② 610
Straight ② 502
Satin ② 822
Chain ② 822
Satin ② 3045
Straight ② 822
Satin ② 502
Chain ② 422

257
French knot ② 729
French knot ② 918
Satin ② 3023
Outline ② 3053
Satin ② E677
Satin ② 758
Lazy daisy ② 3053
Straight ② 3781
Chain ② 3051

258
Satin ② E677
Chain ② 822
French knot ① 3787
Satin ② 822
Satin ② E677
Satin ② 3821
Satin ② 3053
Chain ② 610

250

251

252

253

254

255

256

257

258

Fairytale Animals

Photo: page 23

- ■ The numbers represent the color numbers for DMC No. 25 embroidery floss
- ■ The numbers in ◯ represent the number of strands of thread
- ■ Wrap French knots twice, unless otherwise noted
- ■ Straight ① 3781 for the eyes and whiskers, unless otherwise noted
- ■ French knot ① 3781 for the noses, unless otherwise noted

259
Chain ② 610
Satin ② 729
Satin ② 822
Satin ② E677
Satin ② 758
Outline ② 3053
Lazy daisy ② 3053
Chain ② 610
French knot ② 918

260
Satin ② 822
Satin ② E677
Satin ② 610
Chain ② 610
Lazy daisy ② 3768
Satin ② 822
Lazy daisy ② 3051
Straight ② 3778
Outline ② 610
Straight ② 3781
Chain ② 451
Outline ② 3051

261
Satin ② 3045
Satin ② E677
Satin ② 502
Chain ② 3787
Straight ② 3781
Chain ② 422

262
Lazy daisy ② 918
Straight ② 3821
Satin ② 822
Lazy daisy ② 918
Satin ② E677
Satin ② 3023
Straight ② 3051
Chain ② 3053

263
Chain ② 502
Lazy daisy ② 3781
Chain ② 822
Satin ② 729
Satin ② 822
Satin ② E677
Satin ② 918
Satin ② 502
Satin ② 822
Chain ② 3781
Straight ② 3781
Satin ② 729

264
Satin ② 3023
Lazy daisy ② E677
Straight ② E677
Satin ② 3045
Chain ② 451

265
Satin ② 3023
Running ① E677
Lazy daisy ② E677
Satin ② 3023
Straight ② E677
Chain ② 918
Satin ② 3768
Straight ② 3781

266
Satin ② 822
Satin ② 422
Satin ② E677
Satin ② 822
Chain ② 3778

267
Outline ② 3023
Straight ① E677
French knot ② 918
Satin ② E677
French knot ② 729
Satin ② 3045
Outline ② 3051
Satin ② E677
Lazy daisy ② 3051
Satin ② 918
Straight ② 3781
Chain ② 610

259

260

261

262

263

264

265

266

267

More Fairytale Animals

STITCH GUIDE

Photo: page 24

- ■ The numbers represent the color numbers for DMC No. 25 embroidery floss
- ■ The numbers in ○ represent the number of strands of thread
- ■ Wrap French knots twice, unless otherwise noted
- ■ Straight ① 3781 for the eyes and whiskers, unless otherwise noted
- ■ French knot ① 3781 for the noses, unless otherwise noted

268
Chain ② 3045
Chain ② 451
Lazy daisy ② 918
Satin ② 822
Satin ② 3051
Satin ② 3053
Straight ② 3821
Straight ② 3781

269
Chain ② 502
Chain ② 3781
Satin ② 822
Satin ② 3045
Straight ② 3051
Lazy daisy ② 918
Satin ② 3053
Satin ② 3787
Satin ② E677

270
Outline ② 3787
Chain ② 451
Satin ② E677
Satin ② 422
Satin ② 3778
Satin ② 422
Satin ② E677
Satin ② 3768

271
Satin ② 422
Satin ② E677
Satin ② 3023
Straight ② 3781
Back ② 822
Chain ② 918
Chain ② 3051
Outline ② 3781
Chain ② 822

272
French knot ① 3781
Chain ② 3045
Chain ② 822
Satin ② E677
Chain ② 451
Chain ② 3053
Chain ② 3051

273
Chain ② 918
Chain ② 451
Chain ② 3768
Satin ② 822
Chain ② 3787
Satin ② E677
Straight ② 3781
Satin ② 729

274
Satin ② 3023
Satin ② 502
Satin ② E677
Chain ② 3781
Outline ② 3023
Chain ② 822
Satin ② 918

275
Chain ② 918
Straight ① E677
Outline ② 822
Lazy daisy ② 918
Straight ② 3821
Chain ② 822
Satin ② 822
Satin ② E677
Satin ② 3051
Chain ② 3045
Straight ② 3781

276
Satin ② 3781
Satin ② 729
Satin ② 918
Outline ② 3781
Satin ② 822
Chain ② 3053
Satin ② E677
Chain ② 502
Chain ② 3778

268

269

270

271

272

273

274

275

276

More Fairytale Animals

Photo: page 25

- The numbers represent the color numbers for DMC No. 25 embroidery floss
- The numbers in ◯ represent the number of strands of thread
- Wrap French knots twice, unless otherwise noted
- Straight ① 3781 for the eyes and whiskers, unless otherwise noted
- French knot ① 3781 for the noses, unless otherwise noted

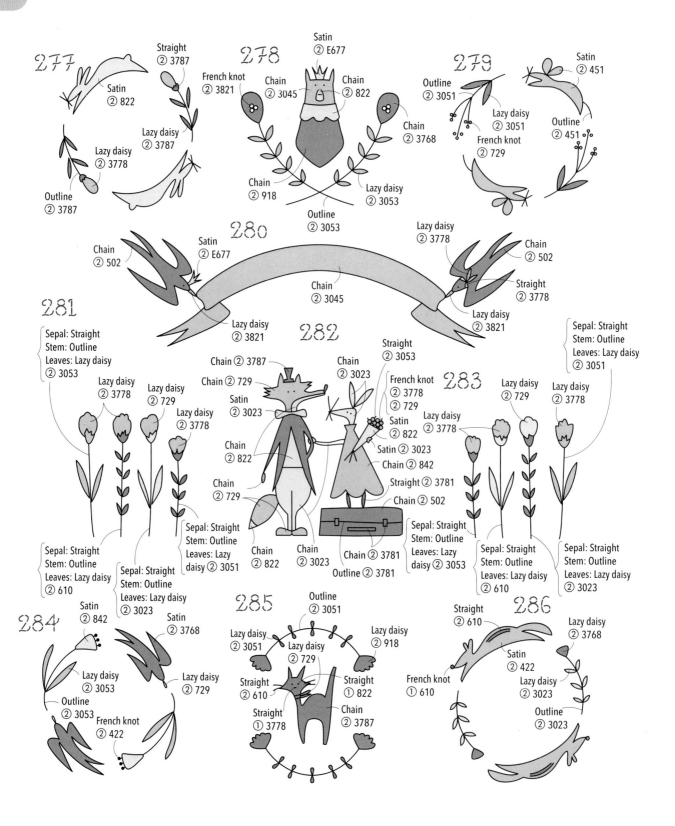

277
Straight ② 3787
Satin ② 822
Lazy daisy ② 3787
Lazy daisy ② 3778
Outline ② 3787

278
Satin ② E677
French knot ② 3821
Chain ② 3045
Chain ② 822
Chain ② 3768
Chain ② 918
Lazy daisy ② 3053
Outline ② 3053

279
Outline ② 3051
Satin ② 451
Lazy daisy ② 3051
Outline ② 451
French knot ② 729

280
Chain ② 502
Satin ② E677
Chain ② 3045
Lazy daisy ② 3778
Chain ② 502
Straight ② 3778
Lazy daisy ② 3821
Lazy daisy ② 3821

281
Sepal: Straight
Stem: Outline
Leaves: Lazy daisy
② 3053
Lazy daisy ② 3778
Lazy daisy ② 729
Lazy daisy ② 3778
Sepal: Straight
Stem: Outline
Leaves: Lazy daisy
② 610
Sepal: Straight
Stem: Outline
Leaves: Lazy daisy
② 3023

282
Chain ② 3787
Chain ② 729
Satin ② 3023
Chain ② 822
Chain ② 729
Chain ② 3023
Straight ② 3053
French knot ② 3778 ② 729
Satin ② 822
Satin ② 3023
Chain ② 842
Straight ② 3781
Chain ② 502
Chain ② 822
Chain ② 3023
Chain ② 3781
Outline ② 3781

283
Lazy daisy ② 729
Lazy daisy ② 3778
Lazy daisy ② 3778
Lazy daisy ② 729
Lazy daisy ② 3778
Sepal: Straight
Stem: Outline
Leaves: Lazy daisy
② 3053
Sepal: Straight
Stem: Outline
Leaves: Lazy daisy
② 610
Sepal: Straight
Stem: Outline
Leaves: Lazy daisy
② 3023
Sepal: Straight
Stem: Outline
Leaves: Lazy daisy
② 3051

284
Satin ② 842
Satin ② 3768
Lazy daisy ② 3053
Lazy daisy ② 729
Outline ② 3053
French knot ② 422

285
Outline ② 3051
Lazy daisy ② 3051
Lazy daisy ② 729
Lazy daisy ② 918
Straight ② 610
Straight ① 822
Straight ① 3778
Chain ② 3787

286
Straight ② 610
Lazy daisy ② 3768
Satin ② 422
French knot ① 610
Lazy daisy ② 3023
Outline ② 3023

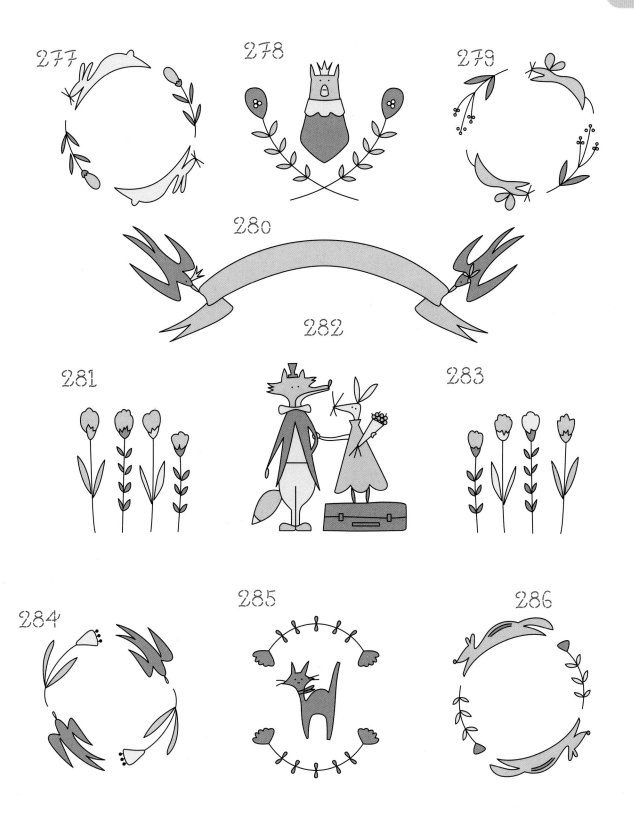

277

278

279

280

282

281

283

284

285

286

Everyday Life

Photo: page 26

■ The numbers represent the color numbers for DMC No. 25 embroidery floss
■ The numbers in ◯ represent the number of strands of thread
■ Wrap French knots twice, unless otherwise noted

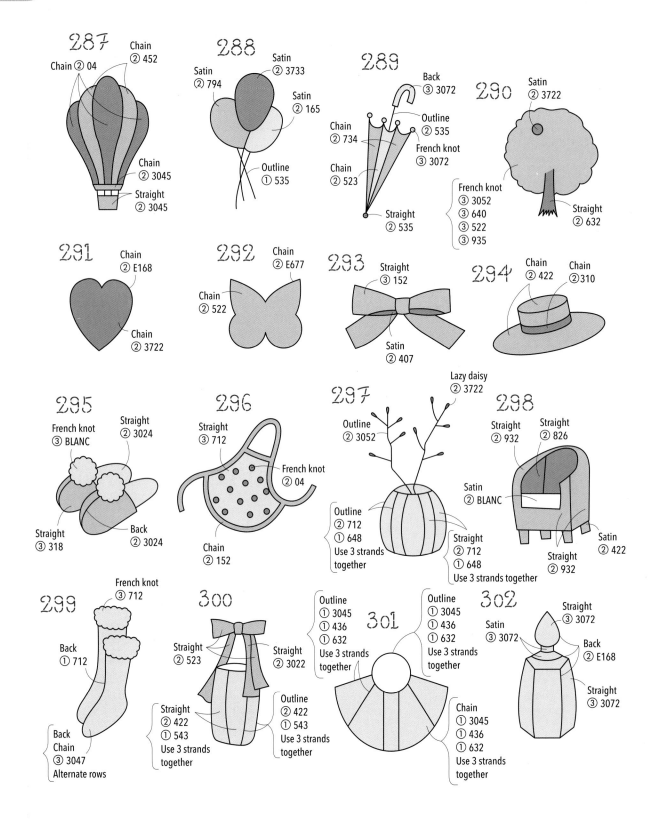

287
Chain ② 04
Chain ② 452
Chain ③ 3045
Straight ② 3045

288
Satin ② 794
Satin ② 3733
Satin ② 165
Outline ① 535

289
Back ③ 3072
Outline ② 535
Chain ② 734
French knot ③ 3072
Chain ② 523
Straight ② 535
French knot ③ 3052 ③ 640 ③ 522 ③ 935

290
Satin ② 3722
French knot ③ 3052 ③ 640 ③ 522 ③ 935
Straight ② 632

291
Chain ② E168
Chain ② 3722

292
Chain ② E677
Chain ② 522

293
Straight ③ 152
Satin ② 407

294
Chain ② 422
Chain ② 310

295
French knot ③ BLANC
Straight ② 3024
Straight ③ 318
Back ② 3024

296
Straight ③ 712
French knot ② 04
Chain ② 152

297
Lazy daisy ② 3722
Outline ② 3052
Outline ② 712 ① 648 Use 3 strands together
Straight ② 712 ① 648 Use 3 strands together

298
Straight ② 932
Straight ② 826
Satin ② BLANC
Straight ② 932
Satin ② 422

299
French knot ③ 712
Back ① 712
Back Chain ③ 3047 Alternate rows

300
Straight ② 523
Straight ② 3022
Straight ② 422 ① 543 Use 3 strands together
Outline ② 422 ① 543 Use 3 strands together

301
Outline ① 3045 ① 436 ① 632 Use 3 strands together
Outline ① 3045 ① 436 ① 632 Use 3 strands together
Chain ① 3045 ① 436 ① 632 Use 3 strands together

302
Straight ③ 3072
Satin ③ 3072
Back ② E168
Straight ③ 3072

287

288

289

290

291

292

293

294

295

296

297

298

299

300

301

302

Everyday Life

Photo: page 27

- The numbers represent the color numbers for DMC No. 25 embroidery floss
- The numbers in ○ represent the number of strands of thread
- Wrap French knots twice, unless otherwise noted

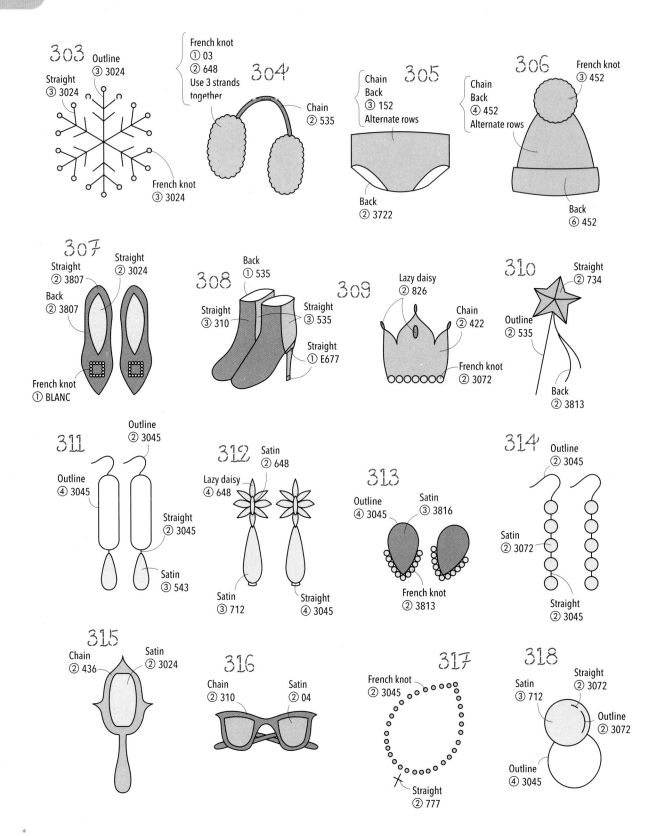

303
Outline ③ 3024
Straight ③ 3024
French knot ③ 3024

304
French knot ① 03 ② 648 Use 3 strands together
Chain ② 535

305
Chain Back ③ 152 Alternate rows
Back ② 3722

306
French knot ③ 452
Chain Back ④ 452 Alternate rows
Back ⑥ 452

307
Straight ② 3807
Straight ② 3024
Back ② 3807
French knot ① BLANC

308
Back ① 535
Straight ③ 310
Straight ③ 535
Straight ① E677

309
Lazy daisy ② 826
Chain ② 422
French knot ② 3072

310
Straight ② 734
Outline ② 535
Back ② 3813

311
Outline ② 3045
Outline ④ 3045
Straight ② 3045
Satin ③ 543

312
Satin ② 648
Lazy daisy ④ 648
Satin ③ 712
Straight ④ 3045

313
Outline ④ 3045
Satin ③ 3816
French knot ② 3813

314
Outline ② 3045
Satin ② 3072
Straight ② 3045

315
Chain ② 436
Satin ② 3024

316
Chain ② 310
Satin ② 04

317
French knot ② 3045
Straight ② 777

318
Satin ③ 712
Straight ② 3072
Outline ② 3072
Outline ④ 3045

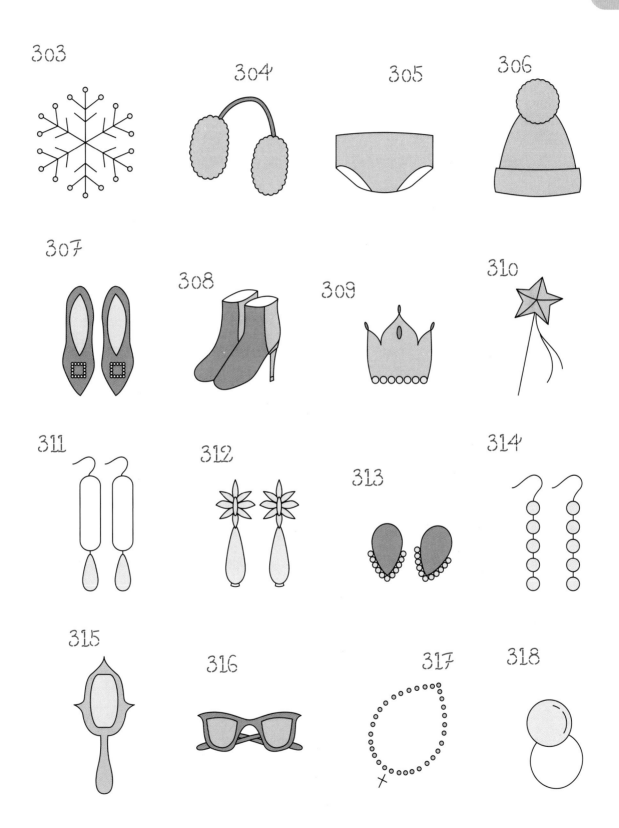

303

304

305

306

307

308

309

310

311

312

313

314

315

316

317

318

Sports & Games

Photo: page 28

- ■ The numbers represent the color numbers for DMC No. 25 embroidery floss
- ■ The numbers in ◯ represent the number of strands of thread
- ■ Wrap French knots twice, unless otherwise noted

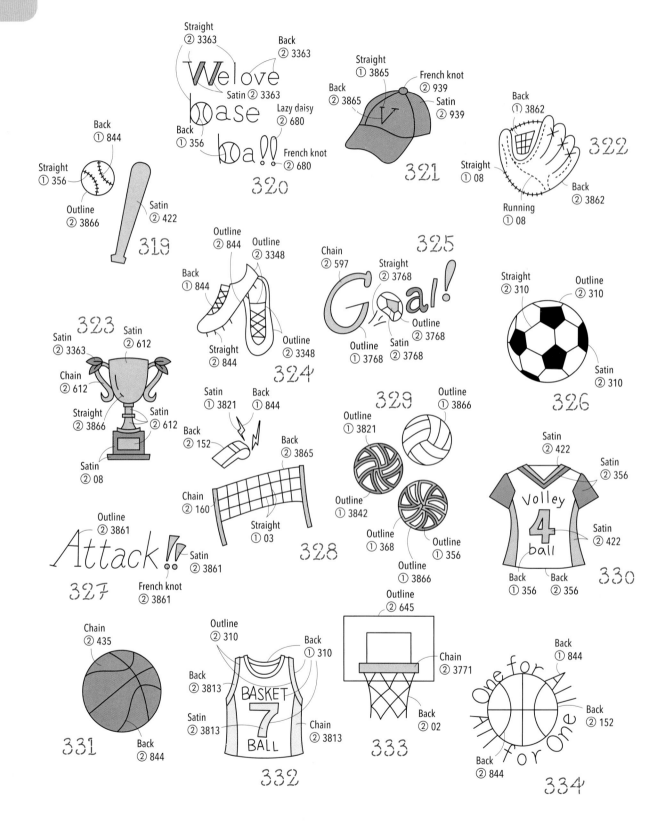

Straight ② 3363
Back ② 3363
Satin ② 3363
Lazy daisy ② 680
Back ① 356
French knot ② 680
We love base ball!!
320

Straight ① 3865
Back ② 3865
French knot ② 939
Satin ② 939
321

Back ① 3862
322
Straight ① 08
Back ② 3862
Running ① 08

Back ① 844
Straight ① 356
Outline ② 3866
Satin ② 422
319

Outline ② 844
Outline ② 3348
Back ① 844
Straight ② 844
Outline ② 3348
324

Chain ② 597
Straight ② 3768
325
Outline ② 3768
Outline ① 3768
Satin ② 3768
Goal!

Straight ② 310
Outline ② 310
Satin ② 310
326

Satin ② 3363
Satin ② 612
Chain ② 612
323
Straight ② 3866
Satin ② 612
Satin ② 08

Satin ① 3821
Back ① 844
Back ② 152
Back ② 3865
Chain ② 160
Straight ① 03
328

Outline ① 3821
329
Outline ① 3866
Outline ① 3842
Outline ① 368
Outline ① 356
Outline ① 3866

Satin ② 422
Satin ② 356
Volley 4 ball
Satin ② 422
Back ① 356
Back ② 356
330

Outline ② 3861
Attack!!
Satin ② 3861
French knot ② 3861
327

Chain ② 435
331
Back ② 844

Outline ② 310
Back ① 310
Back ② 3813
Satin ② 3813
BASKET 7 BALL
Chain ② 3813
332

Outline ② 645
Chain ② 3771
Back ② 02
333

Back ① 844
One for All For one
Back ② 152
Back ② 844
334

We love base ball
320

321

322

319

325

323

Goal!

324

326

329

Attack!!
327

328

Volley 4 ball
330

331

BASKET 7 BALL
332

333

One for All for One
334

Sports & Games

Photo: page 29

- The numbers represent the color numbers for DMC No. 25 embroidery floss
- The numbers in ◯ represent the number of strands of thread
- Wrap French knots twice, unless otherwise noted

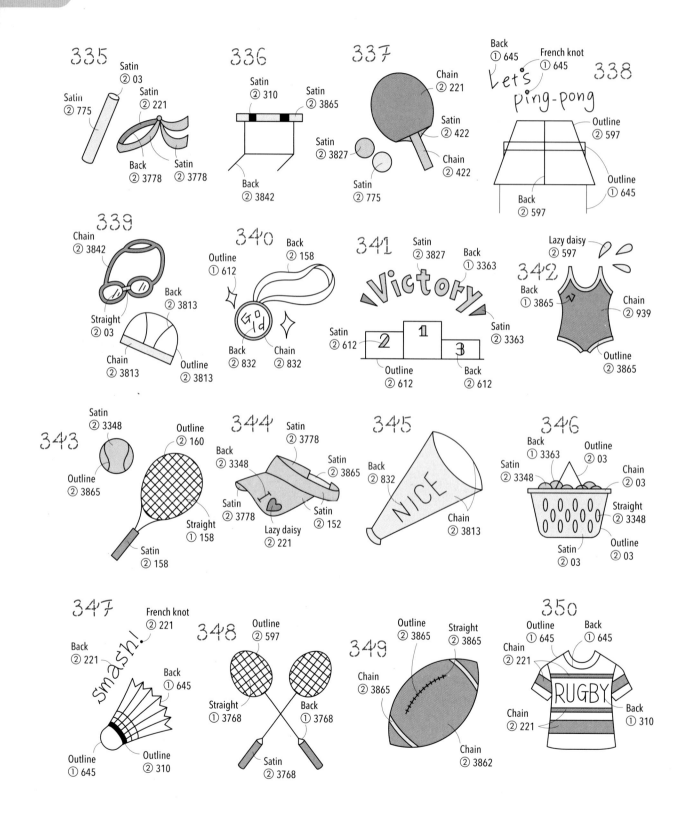

335
Satin ② 03
Satin ② 775
Satin ② 221
Back ② 3778
Satin ② 3778

336
Satin ② 310
Satin ② 3865
Back ② 3842

337
Chain ② 221
Satin ② 422
Satin ② 3827
Chain ② 422
Satin ② 775

338
Back ① 645
French knot ① 645
Let's ping-pong
Outline ② 597
Outline ① 645
Back ② 597

339
Chain ② 3842
Back ② 3813
Straight ② 03
Chain ② 3813
Outline ② 3813

340
Outline ① 612
Back ② 158
Back ② 832
Chain ② 832

341
Satin ② 3827
Back ① 3363
Victory
Satin ② 3363
Satin ② 612
Outline ② 612
Back ② 612

342
Lazy daisy ② 597
Back ① 3865
Chain ② 939
Outline ② 3865

343
Satin ② 3348
Outline ② 160
Outline ② 3865
Straight ① 158
Satin ② 158

344
Satin ② 3778
Back ② 3348
Satin ② 3865
Satin ② 3778
Lazy daisy ② 221
Satin ② 152

345
Back ② 832
NICE
Chain ② 3813

346
Back ① 3363
Outline ② 03
Satin ② 3348
Chain ② 03
Straight ② 3348
Satin ② 03
Outline ② 03

347
French knot ② 221
Back ② 221
smash!
Back ① 645
Outline ① 645
Outline ② 310

348
Outline ② 597
Straight ① 3768
Back ① 3768
Satin ② 3768

349
Outline ② 3865
Straight ② 3865
Chain ② 3865
Chain ② 3862

350
Outline ① 645
Back ① 645
Chain ② 221
RUGBY
Chain ② 221
Back ① 310

335

336

337

Let's
ping-pong 338

339

340

341 Victory

342

343

344

345 NICE

346

347 smash!

348

349

350 RUGBY

Hobbies & Activities

Photo: page 30

- The numbers represent the color numbers for DMC No. 25 embroidery floss
- The numbers in ◯ represent the number of strands of thread
- Wrap French knots twice, unless otherwise noted

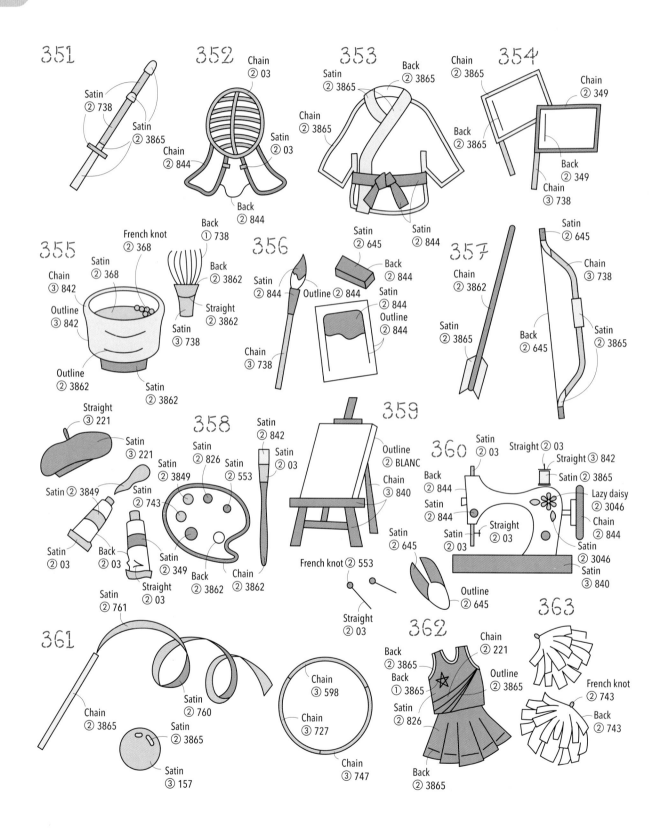

351

Satin ② 738
Satin ② 3865

352

Chain ② 03
Chain ② 844
Satin ② 03
Back ② 844

353

Satin ② 3865
Chain ② 3865
Back ② 3865
Chain ② 3865
Back ② 3865
Satin ② 645
Satin ② 844

354

Chain ② 3865
Chain ② 349
Back ② 349
Chain ③ 738

355

French knot ② 368
Satin ② 368
Chain ③ 842
Outline ③ 842
Outline ② 3862
Back ① 738
Back ② 3862
Straight ② 3862
Satin ③ 738
Satin ③ 3862
Satin ② 3862

356

Satin ② 844
Back ② 844
Outline ② 844
Satin ② 844
Outline ② 844
Chain ③ 738

357

Chain ② 3862
Satin ② 3865
Back ② 645
Satin ② 645
Chain ③ 738
Satin ② 3865

358

Straight ③ 221
Satin ③ 221
Satin ② 3849
Satin ② 3849
Satin ② 743
Satin ② 03
Back ② 03
Satin ② 349
Straight ② 03
Back ② 3862
Satin ② 826
Satin ② 553
Satin ② 842
Satin ② 03
Chain ② 3862
Satin ② 761

359

Outline ② BLANC
Chain ③ 840
Satin ② 645
French knot ② 553
Straight ② 03

360

Satin ② 03
Straight ② 03
Straight ③ 842
Satin ② 3865
Lazy daisy ② 3046
Chain ② 844
Satin ② 3046
Satin ③ 840
Back ② 844
Satin ② 844
Satin ② 03
Straight ② 03
Outline ② 645

361

Chain ② 3865
Satin ② 760
Satin ② 3865
Satin ③ 157

Chain ③ 598
Chain ③ 727
Chain ③ 747

362

Chain ② 221
Back ② 3865
Back ① 3865
Outline ② 3865
Satin ② 826
Back ② 3865

363

French knot ② 743
Back ② 743

351 352 353 354

355 356 357

358 359 360

361 362 363

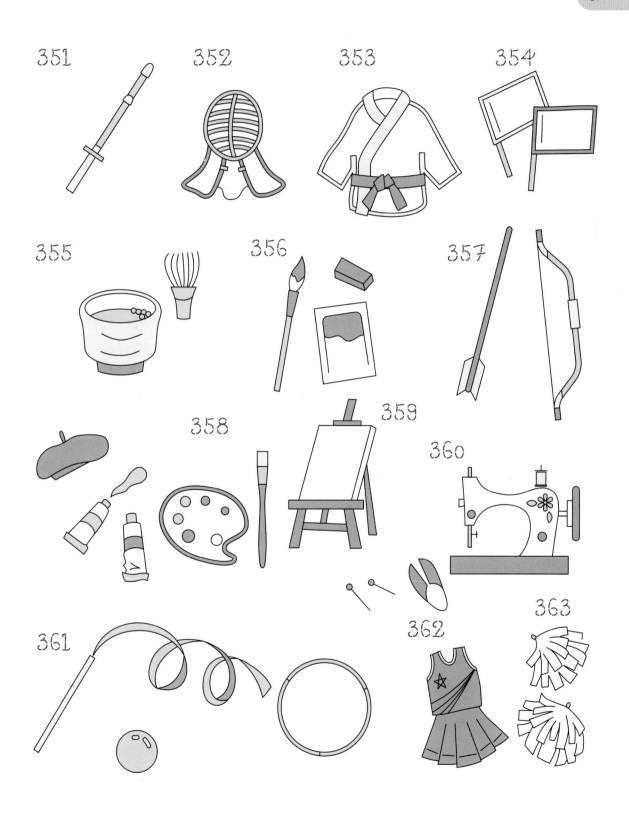

Hobbies & Activities

Photo: page 31

- The numbers represent the color numbers for DMC No. 25 embroidery floss
- The numbers in ◯ represent the number of strands of thread
- Wrap French knots twice, unless otherwise noted

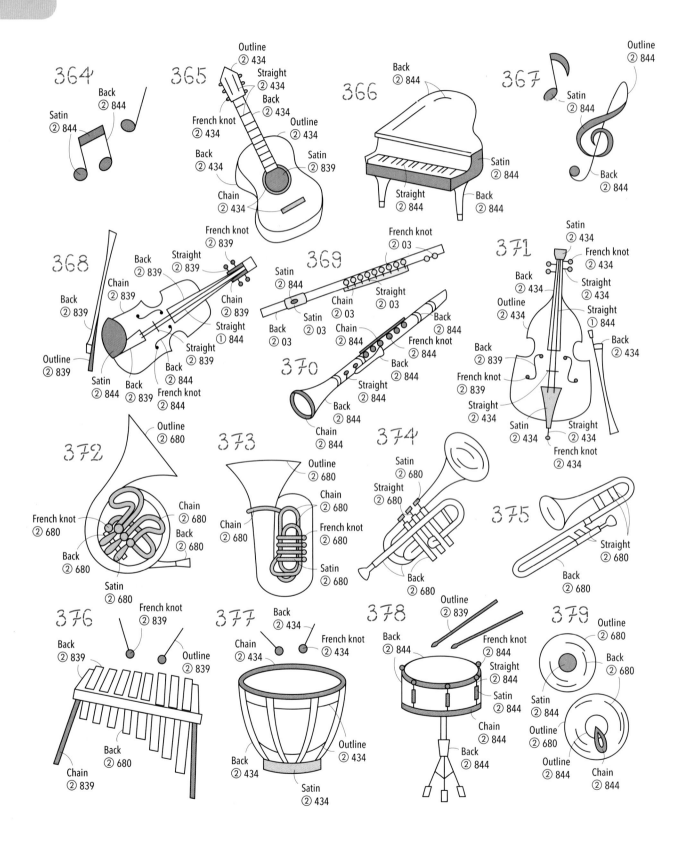

364
Satin ② 844
Back ② 844

365
Outline ② 434
Straight ② 434
Back ② 434
French knot ② 434
Back ② 434
Outline ② 434
Satin ② 839
Chain ② 434

366
Back ② 844
Satin ② 844
Straight ② 844
Back ② 844

367
Outline ② 844
Satin ② 844
Back ② 844

368
French knot ② 839
Back ② 839
Straight ② 839
Chain ② 839
Back ② 839
Chain ② 839
Straight ① 844
Straight ② 839
Back ② 844
Outline ② 839
Satin ② 844
Back ② 839
French knot ② 844

369
French knot ② 03
Satin ② 844
Chain ② 03
Straight ② 03
Satin ② 03
Back ② 03
Chain ② 844
Back ② 844
French knot ② 844
Back ② 844

370
Straight ② 844
Back ② 844
Chain ② 844

371
Satin ② 434
French knot ② 434
Back ② 434
Straight ② 434
Outline ② 434
Straight ① 844
Back ② 839
Back ② 434
French knot ② 839
Straight ② 434
Satin ② 434
Straight ② 434
French knot ② 434

372
Outline ② 680
French knot ② 680
Chain ② 680
Back ② 680
Back ② 680
Satin ② 680

373
Outline ② 680
Chain ② 680
Chain ② 680
French knot ② 680
Satin ② 680

374
Satin ② 680
Straight ② 680
Back ② 680

375
Straight ② 680
Back ② 680

376
French knot ② 839
Back ② 839
Outline ② 839
Back ② 680
Chain ② 839

377
Back ② 434
Chain ② 434
French knot ② 434
Outline ② 434
Back ② 434
Satin ② 434

378
Outline ② 839
Back ② 844
French knot ② 844
Straight ② 844
Satin ② 844
Chain ② 844
Back ② 844

379
Outline ② 680
Back ② 680
Satin ② 844
Outline ② 680
Outline ② 844
Chain ② 844

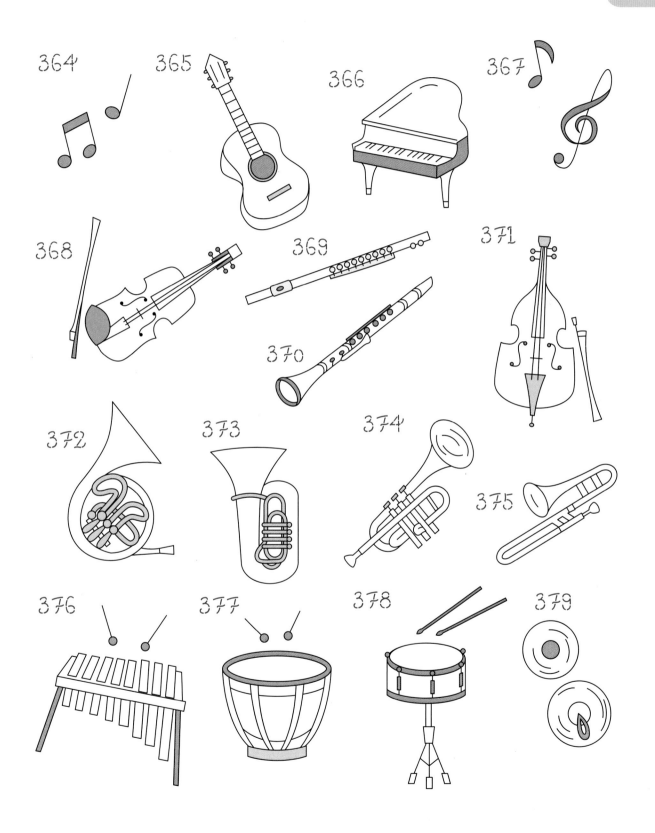

364

365

366

367

368

369

370

371

372

373

374

375

376

377

378

379

Border Designs

Photo: page 32

- The numbers represent the color numbers for DMC No. 25 embroidery floss
- The numbers in ◯ represent the number of strands of thread
- Wrap French knots twice, unless otherwise noted

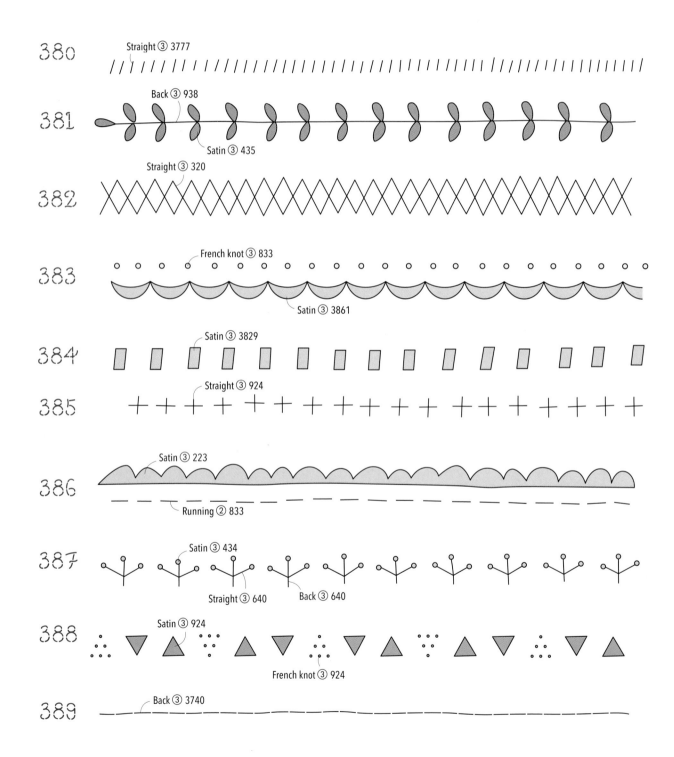

380 — Straight ③ 3777

381 — Back ③ 938 / Satin ③ 435

382 — Straight ③ 320

383 — French knot ③ 833 / Satin ③ 3861

384 — Satin ③ 3829

385 — Straight ③ 924

386 — Satin ③ 223 / Running ② 833

387 — Satin ③ 434 / Straight ③ 640 / Back ③ 640

388 — Satin ③ 924 / French knot ③ 924

389 — Back ③ 3740

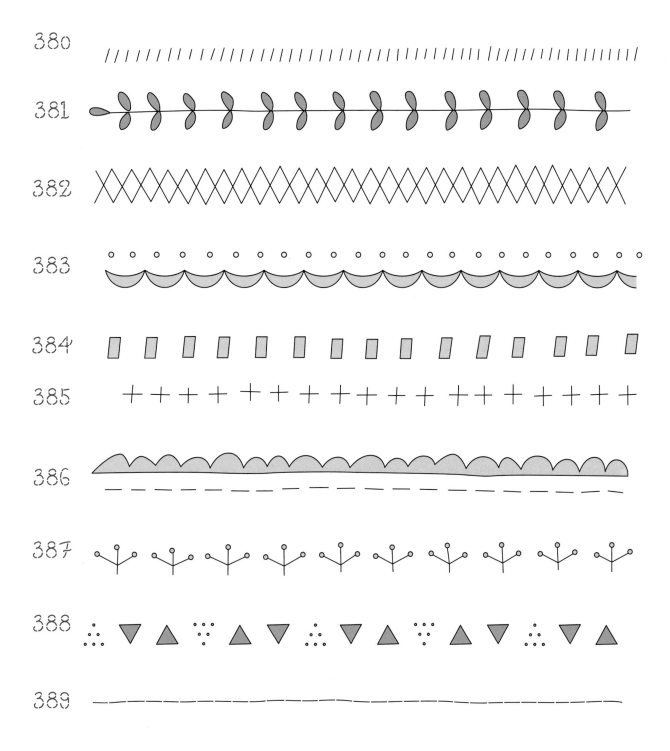

380

381

382

383

384

385

386

387

388

389

Border Designs

Photo: page 33

- ■ The numbers represent the color numbers for DMC No. 25 embroidery floss
- ■ The numbers in ◯ represent the number of strands of thread
- ■ Wrap French knots twice, unless otherwise noted

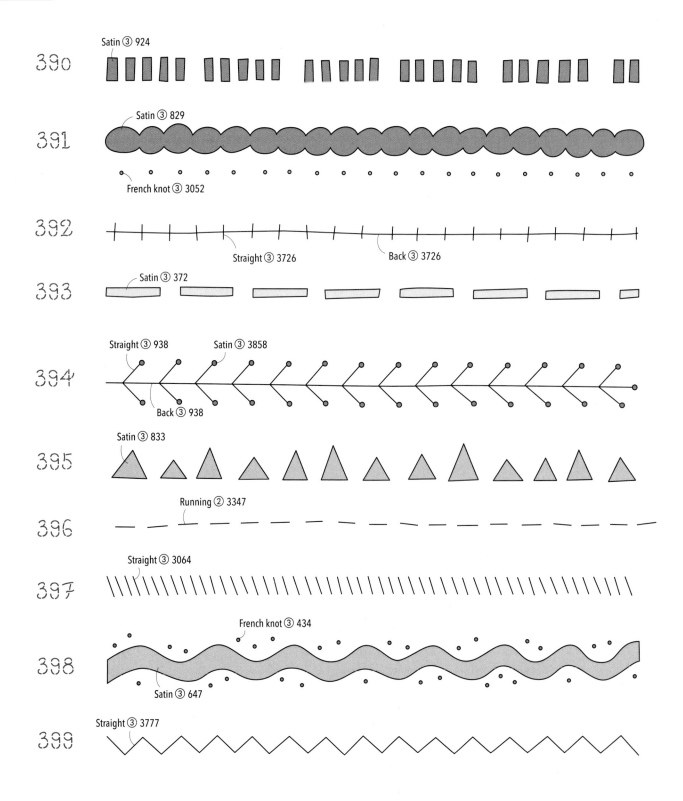

390 — Satin ③ 924

391 — Satin ③ 829 / French knot ③ 3052

392 — Straight ③ 3726 / Back ③ 3726

393 — Satin ③ 372

394 — Straight ③ 938 / Satin ③ 3858 / Back ③ 938

395 — Satin ③ 833

396 — Running ② 3347

397 — Straight ③ 3064

398 — French knot ③ 434 / Satin ③ 647

399 — Straight ③ 3777

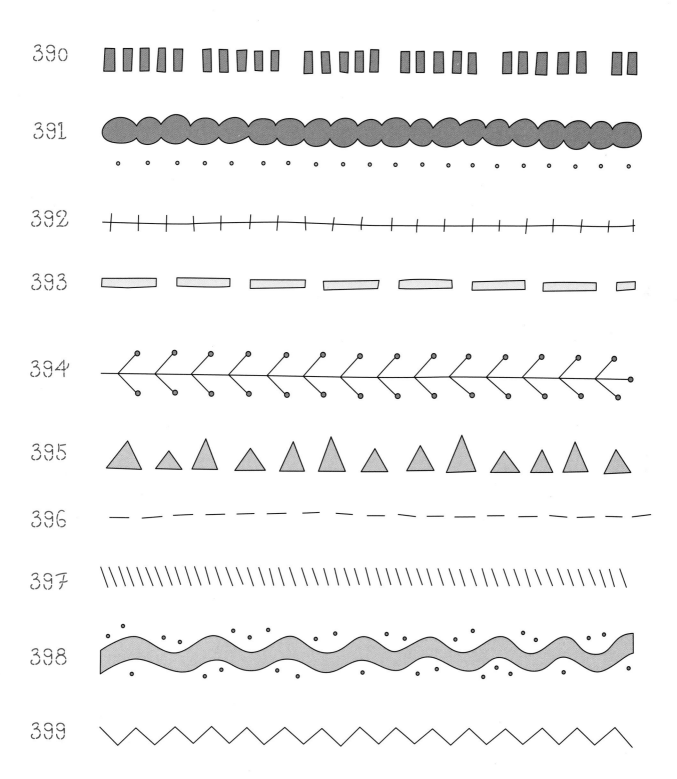

390

391

392

393

394

395

396

397

398

399

Flower Alphabets

Photo: page 34

- The numbers represent the color numbers for Cosmo No. 25 embroidery floss
- The numbers in ◯ represent the number of strands of thread
- Wrap French knots twice, unless otherwise noted

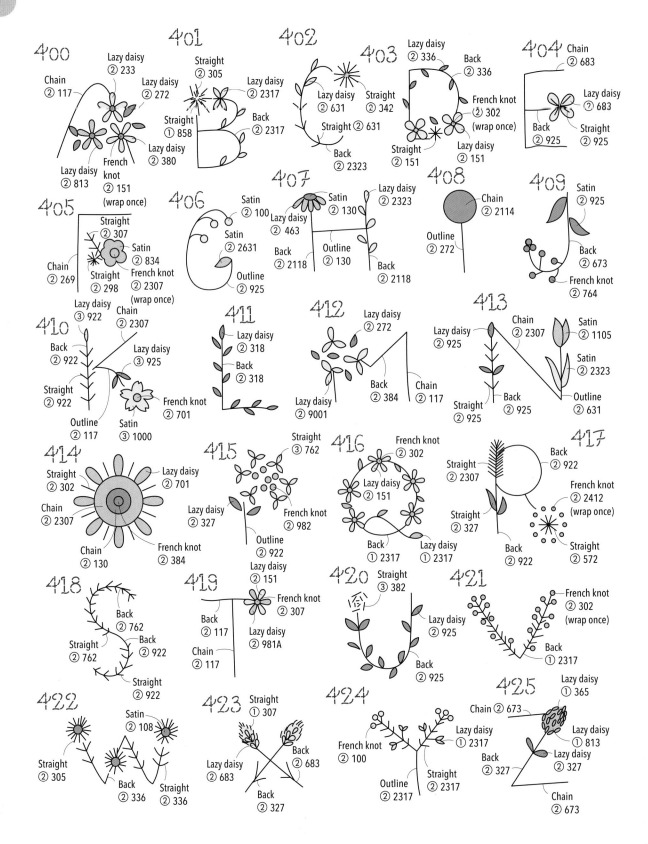

400
Chain ② 117
Lazy daisy ② 233
Lazy daisy ② 272
Lazy daisy ② 813
French knot ② 151 (wrap once)
Lazy daisy ② 380

401
Straight ② 305
Lazy daisy ② 2317
Straight ① 858
Back ② 2317

402
Lazy daisy ② 631
Straight ② 631
Back ② 2323

403
Lazy daisy ② 336
Straight ② 342
Back ② 336
French knot ② 302 (wrap once)
Straight ② 151
Lazy daisy ② 151

404
Chain ② 683
Lazy daisy ② 683
Back ② 925
Straight ② 925

405
Straight ② 307
Satin ② 834
French knot ② 2307 (wrap once)
Chain ② 269
Straight ② 298

406
Satin ② 100
Satin ② 2631
Outline ② 925

407
Satin ② 130
Lazy daisy ② 463
Lazy daisy ② 2323
Back ② 2118
Outline ② 130
Back ② 2118

408
Chain ② 2114
Outline ② 272

409
Satin ② 925
Back ② 673
French knot ② 764

410
Lazy daisy ③ 922
Chain ② 2307
Back ② 922
Lazy daisy ③ 925
Straight ② 922
Outline ② 117
Satin ③ 1000
French knot ② 701

411
Lazy daisy ② 318
Back ② 318

412
Lazy daisy ② 272
Back ② 384
Chain ② 117
Lazy daisy ② 9001

413
Chain ② 2307
Satin ② 1105
Satin ② 2323
Straight ② 925
Back ② 925
Outline ② 631
Lazy daisy ② 925

414
Straight ② 302
Lazy daisy ② 701
Chain ② 2307
Chain ② 130
French knot ② 384

415
Straight ③ 762
Lazy daisy ② 327
Outline ② 922
Lazy daisy ② 151
French knot ② 982

416
French knot ② 302
Lazy daisy ② 151
Back ① 2317
Lazy daisy ① 2317

417
Back ② 922
Straight ② 2307
Straight ② 327
Back ② 922
French knot ② 2412 (wrap once)
Straight ② 572

418
Back ② 762
Straight ② 762
Back ② 922
Straight ② 922

419
Back ② 117
Chain ② 117
French knot ② 307
Lazy daisy ② 981A

420
Straight ③ 382
Lazy daisy ② 925
Back ② 925

421
French knot ② 302 (wrap once)
Back ① 2317

422
Satin ② 108
Straight ② 305
Back ② 336
Straight ② 336

423
Straight ① 307
Lazy daisy ② 683
Back ② 683
Back ② 327

424
French knot ② 100
Lazy daisy ① 2317
Straight ② 2317
Outline ② 2317

425
Chain ② 673
Lazy daisy ① 365
Lazy daisy ① 813
Lazy daisy ② 327
Back ② 327
Chain ② 673

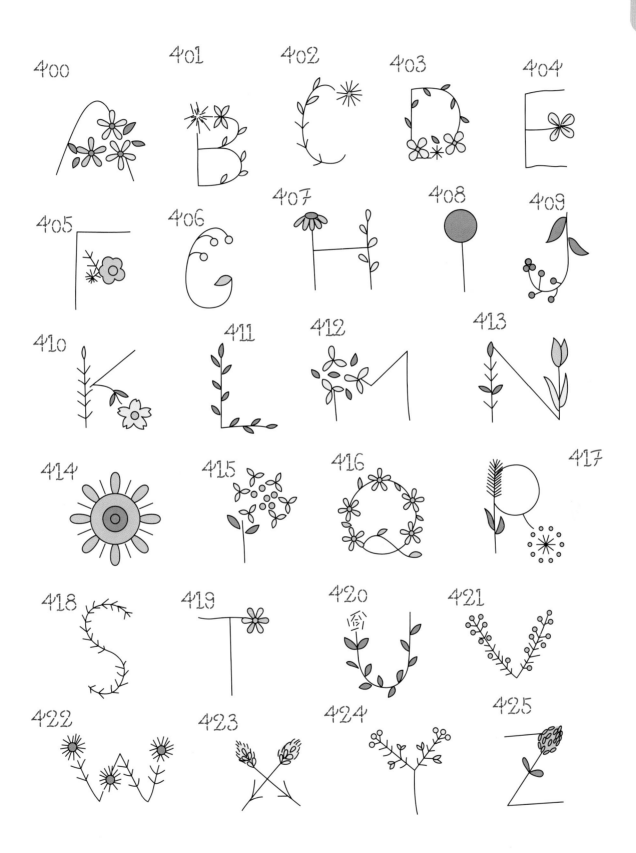

400 401 402 403 404
405 406 407 408 409
410 411 412 413
414 415 416 417
418 419 420 421
422 423 424 425

Flower Alphabets

Photo: page 35

- The numbers represent the color numbers for Cosmo No. 25 embroidery floss
- The numbers in ◯ represent the number of strands of thread
- Wrap French knots twice, unless otherwise noted

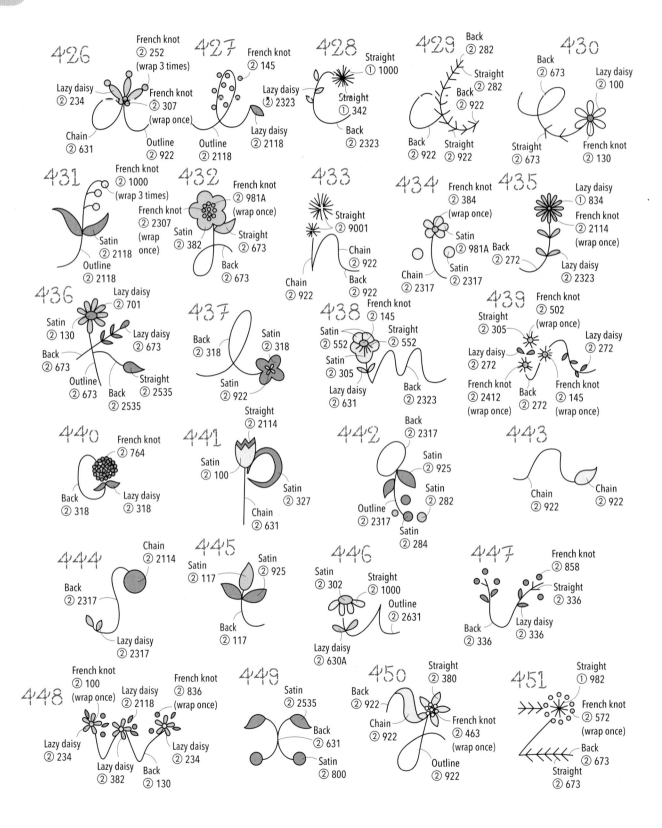

426
French knot
② 252
(wrap 3 times)
French knot
② 307
(wrap once)
Lazy daisy
② 234
Chain
② 631
Outline
② 922

427
French knot
② 145
Lazy daisy
② 2323
Outline
② 2118
Lazy daisy
② 2118

428
Straight
① 1000
Straight
① 342
Back
② 2323

429
Back
② 282
Straight
② 282
Back
② 922
Back
② 922
Straight
② 922

430
Back
② 673
Lazy daisy
② 100
Straight
② 673
French knot
② 130

431
French knot
② 1000
(wrap 3 times)
French knot
② 2307
(wrap once)
Satin
② 2118
Outline
② 2118

432
French knot
② 981A
(wrap once)
Satin
② 382
Straight
② 673
Back
② 673

433
Straight
② 9001
Chain
② 922
Back
② 922
Chain
② 922

434
French knot
② 384
(wrap once)
Satin
② 981A
Satin
② 2317
Chain
② 2317

435
Lazy daisy
① 834
French knot
② 2114
(wrap once)
Lazy daisy
② 2323
Back
② 272

436
Lazy daisy
② 701
Satin
② 130
Lazy daisy
② 673
Back
② 673
Outline
② 673
Straight
② 2535
Back
② 2535

437
Satin
② 318
Back
② 318
Satin
② 922

438
French knot
② 145
Satin
② 552
Straight
② 552
Satin
② 305
Lazy daisy
② 631
Back
② 2323

439
French knot
② 502
(wrap once)
Straight
② 305
Lazy daisy
② 272
Lazy daisy
② 272
French knot
② 2412
(wrap once)
Back
② 272
French knot
② 145
(wrap once)

440
French knot
② 764
Back
② 318
Lazy daisy
② 318

441
Straight
② 2114
Satin
② 100
Satin
② 327
Chain
② 631

442
Back
② 2317
Satin
② 925
Satin
② 282
Outline
② 2317
Satin
② 284

443
Chain
② 922
Chain
② 922

444
Chain
② 2114
Back
② 2317
Lazy daisy
② 2317

445
Satin
② 117
Satin
② 925
Back
② 117

446
Satin
② 302
Straight
② 1000
Outline
② 2631
Lazy daisy
② 630A

447
French knot
② 858
Straight
② 336
Back
② 336
Lazy daisy
② 336

448
French knot
② 100
(wrap once)
Lazy daisy
② 2118
French knot
② 836
(wrap once)
Lazy daisy
② 234
Lazy daisy
② 234
Lazy daisy
② 382
Back
② 130

449
Satin
② 2535
Back
② 631
Satin
② 800

450
Straight
② 380
Back
② 922
Chain
② 922
French knot
② 463
(wrap once)
Outline
② 922

451
Straight
① 982
French knot
② 572
(wrap once)
Back
② 673
Straight
② 673

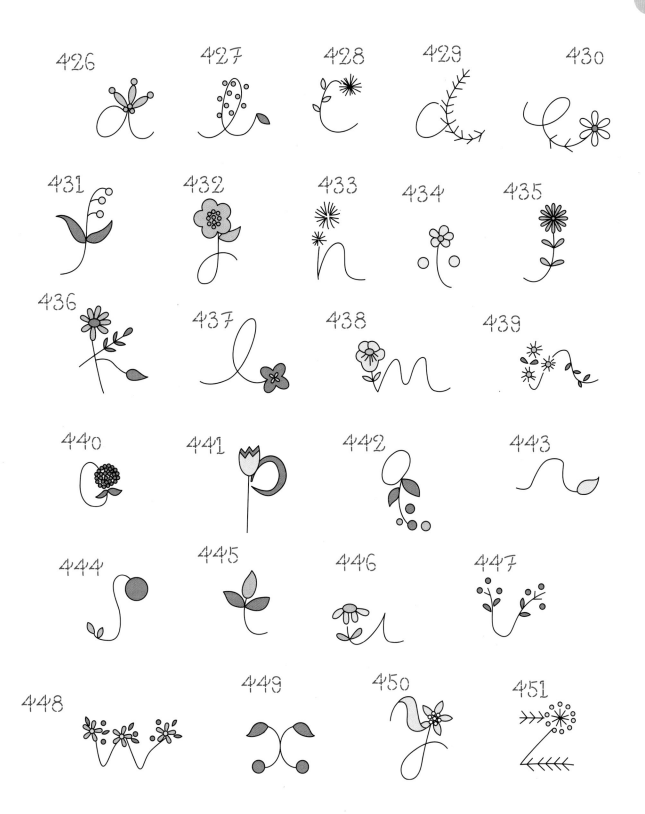

426 427 428 429 430
431 432 433 434 435
436 437 438 439
440 441 442 443
444 445 446 447
448 449 450 451

Food Alphabets

Photo: page 36

- Use Cosmo No. 25 embroidery floss in 310
- The numbers in ○ represent the number of strands of thread
- Wrap French knots twice, unless otherwise noted

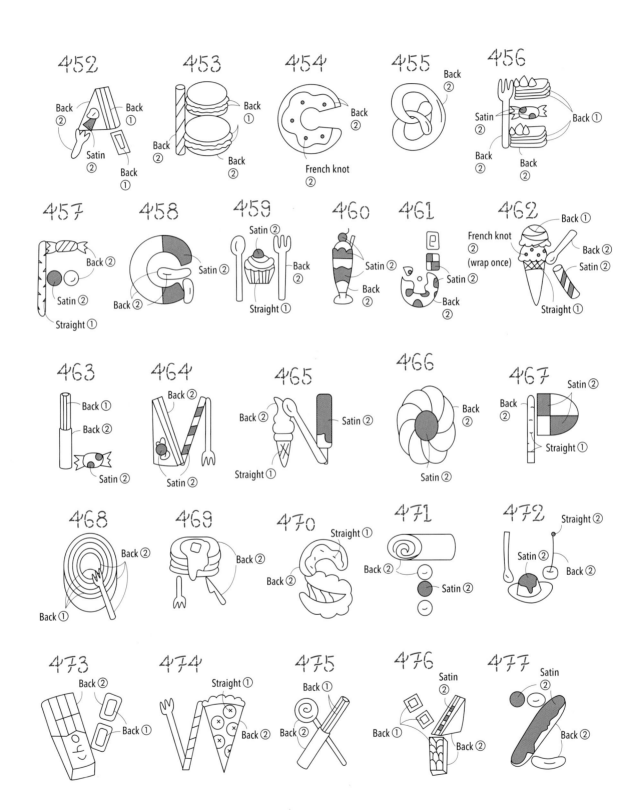

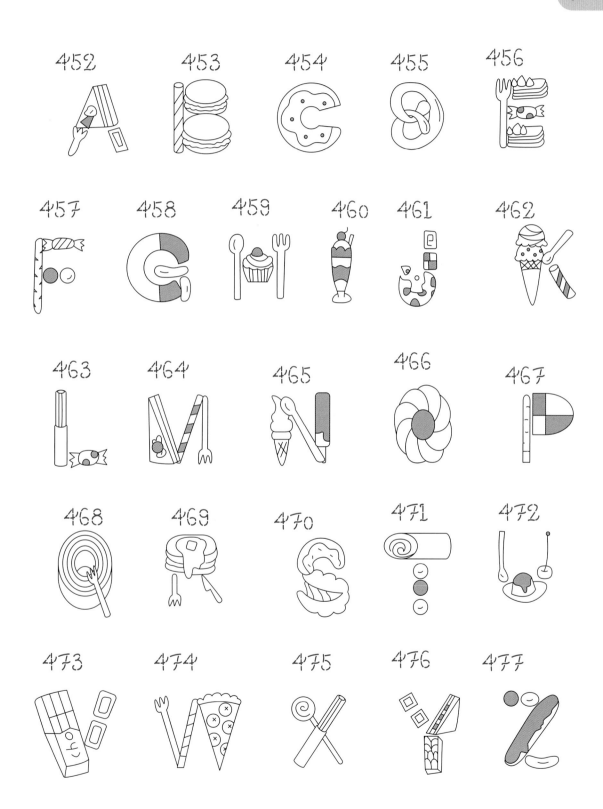

Food Alphabets

Photo: page 37

- Use Cosmo No. 25 embroidery floss in 236
- The numbers in ◯ represent the number of strands of thread
- Wrap French knots twice, unless otherwise noted

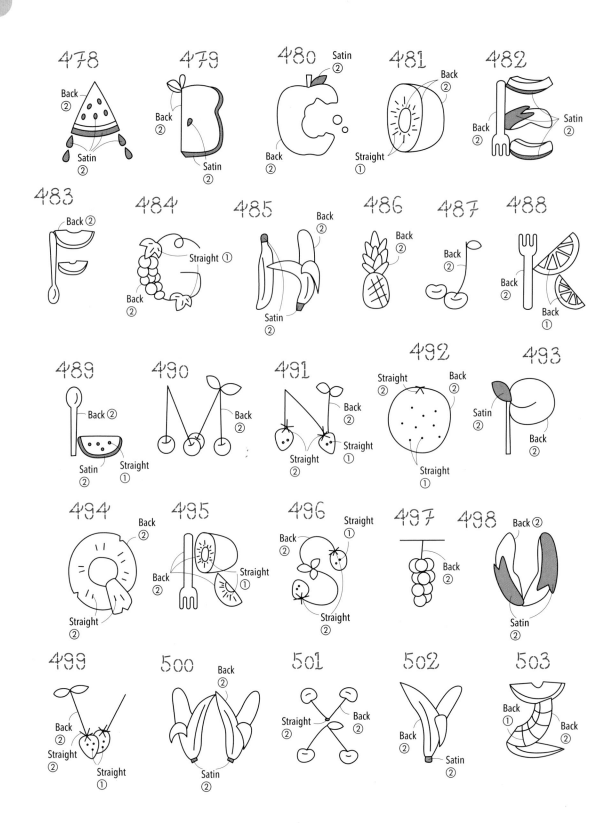

478   479   480   481   482

483   484   485   486   487   488

489   490   491   492   493

494   495   496   497   498

499   500   501   502   503

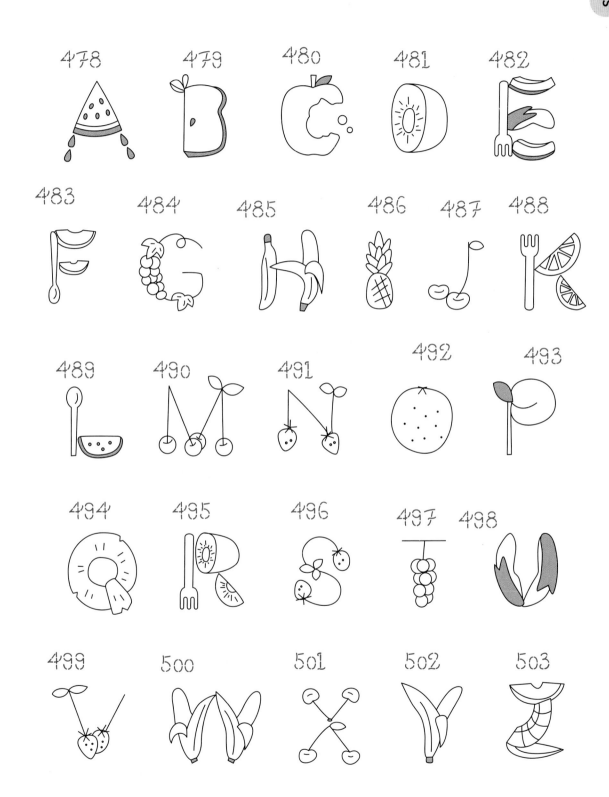

Letters & Numbers

Photo: page 38

- ■ The numbers represent the color numbers for Cosmo No. 25 embroidery floss
- ■ The numbers in ◯ represent the number of strands of thread

504
A B C D E F G
Outline ② 685
C — Straight ② 685
Outline ② 685
Outline ② 685
F — Straight ② 685
Outline ② 685

H I J K L M N
Outline ② 685
J — Back ② 685
Outline ② 685
K — Straight ② 685
Outline ② 685
Outline ② 685
N — Back ② 685

O P Q R S T U
Lazy daisy ② 685
Outline ② 685
Back ② 685
Outline ② 685
Outline ② 685
Outline ② 685
U — Back ② 685
Straight ② 685

V W X Y Z
Outline ② 685
Straight ② 685
Outline ② 685
Outline ② 685
Z — Back ② 685

505
0 1 2 3 4
Straight ① 368
Back ① 368
Outline ② 368
Outline ② 368
Outline ② 368
Straight ① 368
Back ① 368

5 6 7 8 9
Outline ② 368
Straight ① 368
Back ① 368
Outline ② 368
Straight ① 368
Back ① 368
Outline ② 368
Outline ② 368

506
a b c d e f g
Outline ② 576
Satin ② 576
Outline ② 576
Outline ② 576
Outline ② 576

h i j k l m n
Straight ② 576
Outline ② 576
French knot ② 576 (wrap once)
French knot ② 576 (wrap once)
Outline ② 576
Back ② 576
Outline ② 576
Back ② 576
Outline ② 576
Straight ② 576

o p q r s t u
Outline ② 576
Back ② 576
Straight ② 576
Outline ② 576
Outline ② 576
Satin ② 576
Outline ② 576
Back ② 576
Satin ② 576

v w x y z
Back ② 576
Outline ② 576
Outline ② 576
Back ② 576
Outline ② 576

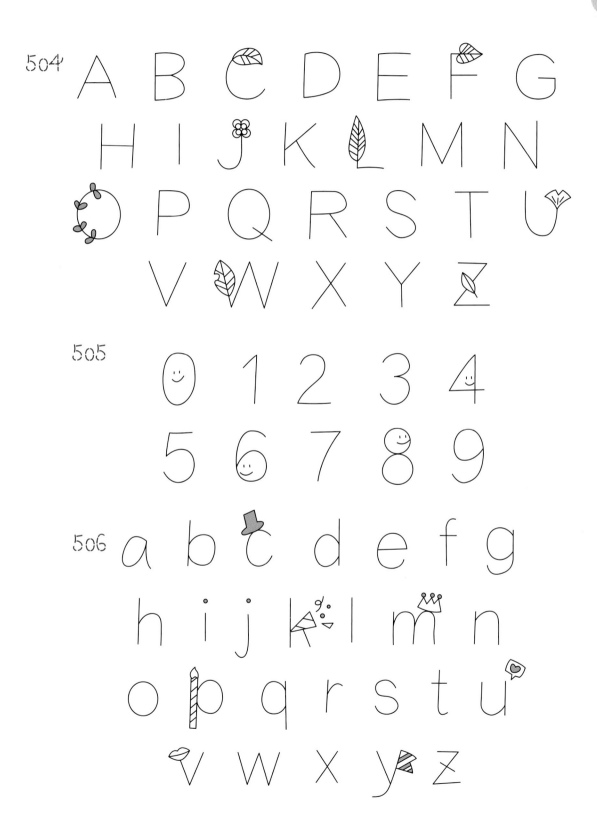

504 A B C D E F G
H I J K L M N
O P Q R S T U
V W X Y Z

505 0 1 2 3 4
5 6 7 8 9

506 a b c d e f g
h i j k l m n
o p q r s t u
v w x y z

Childhood Favorites

Photo: page 39

- The numbers represent the color numbers for DMC No. 25 embroidery floss
- The numbers in ◯ represent the number of strands of thread
- Wrap French knots twice, unless otherwise noted

507
- Outline ③ 535
- Chain ③ 775
- Straight ② 535
- Chain ③ 727
- Chain ③ 817
- Outline ④ 05
- Chain ③ 535

508
- Chain ③ 817
- Chain ③ 3865
- Chain ③ 775
- Chain ③ 727
- Chain ③ 535
- Chain ③ 727
- Chain ③ 310

509
- Chain ③ 817
- Chain ③ 775
- Chain ③ 712
- Chain ③ 535
- Chain ③ 817

510
- Chain ③ 775
- Chain ③ 3866
- Chain ③ 535
- Chain ③ 3051

511
- Straight ③ 535
- Chain ③ 3053
- Chain ③ 677
- Outline ② 535
- Straight ② 535
- Chain ③ 310

512
- Straight ④ 3865
- Chain ③ 775
- Chain ③ 727
- Chain ③ 817

513
- Outline ③ 3853
- Chain ③ 775
- Chain ③ 3853
- Chain ③ 535
- Chain ③ 725
- Chain ③ 535

514
- Outline ③ 823
- Chain ③ 775
- Chain ③ 322
- Chain ③ 727
- Chain ③ 310
- Chain ③ 535

515
- Straight ③ 775
- Outline ③ 823
- Chain ③ 535
- Outline ③ 932

516
- Chain ③ 334
- Back ③ 3865
- Chain ③ 334
- Outline ③ 415

517
- Outline ③ 310
- Chain ③ 310
- Chain ③ 817
- Outline ③ 310

518
- Outline ③ 3371
- Chain ③ 3371

519
- Chain ② 310
- Chain ② 414

520
- Outline ③ 535
- French knot ③ 535
- Outline ③ 712
- Outline ③ 156

521
- Chain French knot ③ 712
- Chain ③ 310

522
- Chain ③ 839
- Outline ③ 415
- Chain ③ 935
- Back ③ 415
- French knot ③ 05
- Chain ③ 839
- Chain ③ 05

507   508   509   510

511   512   513   514

515   516   517   518

519   520   521   522

People & Things

Photo: page 40

■ The numbers represent the color numbers for Olympus No. 25 embroidery floss
■ The numbers in ◯ represent the number of strands of thread
■ Wrap French knots twice, unless otherwise noted

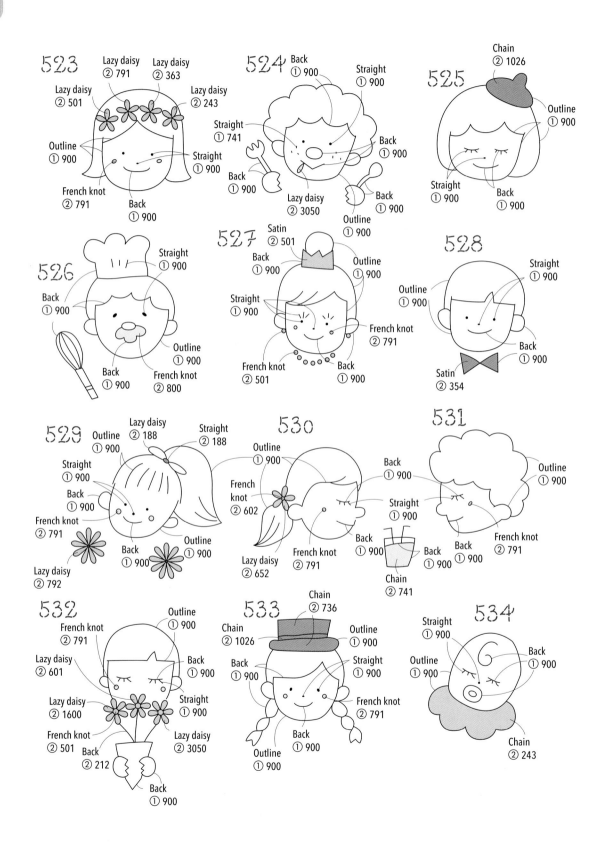

523

524

525

526

527

528

529

530

531

532

533

534

People & Things

Photo: page 41

- ■ The numbers represent the color numbers for Olympus No. 25 embroidery floss
- ■ The numbers in ◯ represent the number of strands of thread
- ■ Wrap French knots twice, unless otherwise noted

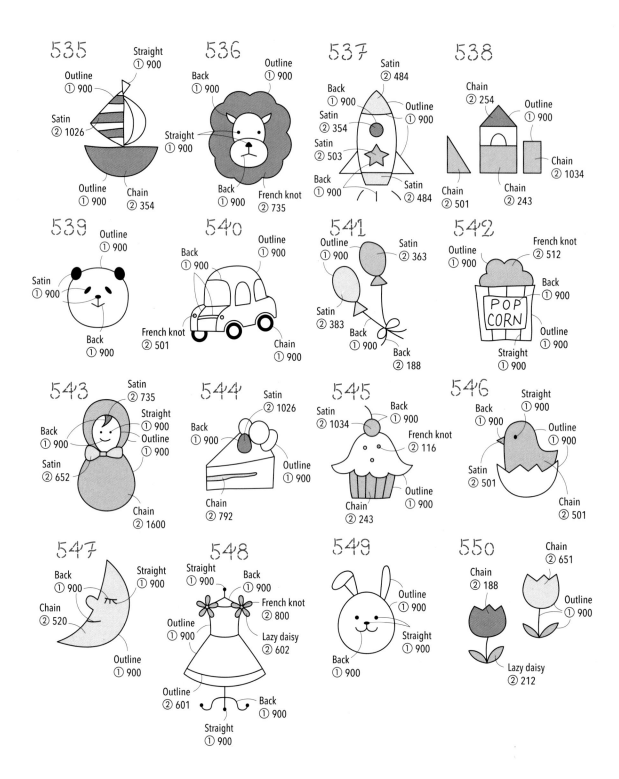

535
Straight ① 900
Outline ① 900
Satin ② 1026
Outline ① 900
Chain ② 354

536
Back ① 900
Outline ① 900
Straight ① 900
Back ① 900
French knot ② 735

537
Satin ② 484
Back ① 900
Outline ① 900
Satin ② 354
Satin ② 503
Back ① 900
Satin ② 484

538
Chain ② 254
Outline ① 900
Chain ② 1034
Chain ② 501
Chain ② 243

539
Outline ① 900
Satin ① 900
Back ① 900

540
Back ① 900
Outline ① 900
French knot ② 501
Chain ① 900

541
Outline ① 900
Satin ② 363
Satin ② 383
Back ① 900
Back ② 188

542
Outline ① 900
French knot ② 512
Back ① 900
Outline ① 900
Straight ① 900

543
Satin ② 735
Straight ① 900
Back ① 900
Outline ① 900
Satin ② 652
Chain ② 1600

544
Satin ② 1026
Back ① 900
Outline ① 900
Chain ② 792

545
Satin ② 1034
Back ① 900
French knot ② 116
Outline ① 900
Chain ② 243

546
Back ① 900
Straight ① 900
Outline ① 900
Satin ② 501
Chain ② 501

547
Back ① 900
Straight ① 900
Chain ② 520
Outline ① 900

548
Straight ① 900
Back ① 900
French knot ② 800
Outline ① 900
Lazy daisy ② 602
Outline ② 601
Back ① 900
Outline ① 900
Straight ① 900

549
Outline ① 900
Straight ① 900
Back ① 900

550
Chain ② 651
Chain ② 188
Outline ① 900
Lazy daisy ② 212

535 536 537 538

539 540 541 542

543 544 545 546

547 548 549 550

Embroidery Artist Profiles

nekogao p. 6–7, 12–13

nekogao is a cat embroidery artist known for making small cloth items, such as brooches, embroidered with cat motifs.

 @nekogao__

nico./Emi Okuda p. 8–9, 32–33

Emi Okuda of nico. loved sewing as a child, so she taught herself how to embroider. She is known for her warm embroidery style and enjoys stitching plant motifs and making beaded accessories.

 @nico.originalhandmade

ironna happa/Shirai Kazumi p. 10–11

Shirai Kazumi of ironna happa works with linen cloth and embroidery thread to create beautiful stitchery. She has participated in a variety of special events and exhibitions, held workshops, and contributed to books and magazines.

 @ironnahappa

pulpy₀/Hisae Hayakawa p. 14–15

Hisae Hayakawa of pulpy₀ strives to incorporate kindness into her work and enjoys stitching animal and food motifs to create handmade accessories. She holds workshops and exhibits and sells her handmade goods.

 @pulpyiii

Chicchi/Chisato & Misato Matsumoto p. 16–19, 28–31

Chicchi is a team of twin sisters named Chisato & Misato who create whimsical animal embroidery featuring adorable characters that inspire you to imagine a fairytale world. Check out their animal embroidery videos on Youtube.

@chicchi_chimi

mopsi p. 20–21

mopsi embroiders brooches and earrings designed to make your day a little more special. She sells her work online and in boutiques around Japan.

 @_mopsi

arinocosha/Alisa Yamaguchi p. 22–25

Alisa Yamaguchi learned needlework at a young age from her grandmother who was a fashion instructor. She launched her embroidery brand arinocosha in 2014 and sells her work throughout Japan. Visit her website at www.arinocosha.com.

@arinocosha

TRÈS JOLIE/Misa Nakano p. 26–27

Trés Jolie, which means "very beautiful" in French, produces embroidered baby goods and fashion accessories that combine basic techniques with original touches. The brand has exhibited at many special events and stores.

@tresjolie_embroidery

Ray chel* /Seiko Yoshihara p. 34–35

Launched in 2017, Ray chel* is an embroidery brand known for customized kid's embroidery featuring names and sayings. Seiko Yoshihara, the brand's creator, is active as an embroidery class instructor in Japan.

@raychel.jp

Kumamori p. 36–38

Kumamori is a self-taught embroidery artist known for her simple and playful designs that inspire nostalgic memories.

kumamori_em

mona.yu p. 40–41

mona.yu started embroidering after becoming inspired to make something for her children. She specializes in embroidered bibs and drawstring pouches.

@mona.yu7

meiP p. 39

meiP is a mother and daughter team that embroiders accessories for kids and babies.

@meip_ig